The Future of Cybersecurity

Guarding the Digital Frontier: Strategies, Tools, and Best Practices

Emily Foster

Table of Contents

INTRODUCTION

In an era where our lives are increasingly intertwined with digital technologies, the importance of cybersecurity cannot be overstated. "The Future of Cybersecurity: Guarding the Digital Frontier: Strategies, Tools, and Best Practices" delves into the complex and ever-evolving landscape of cybersecurity, offering insights, strategies, and practical guidance for navigating the digital frontier.

This book begins with an exploration of the historical evolution of cybersecurity, tracing its roots from the early days of computing to the sophisticated defense mechanisms in place today. It then addresses modern systems' myriad threats and vulnerabilities, from ransomware to advanced persistent threats, and highlights the human element's critical role in cybersecurity.

Readers will find not just theoretical concepts, but comprehensive strategies for developing robust cybersecurity frameworks, leveraging cutting-edge defensive technologies, and securing cloud environments and IoT ecosystems. The book also emphasizes the importance of regulatory compliance and legal considerations, providing a roadmap for organizations to navigate the complex web of cybersecurity laws.

Building a culture of cybersecurity awareness is another key focus, underscoring the need for continuous education and leadership engagement. Finally, the book looks ahead, predicting future threats and exploring innovations in cyber defense while advocating for global collaboration to build a resilient cybersecurity landscape.

CHAPTER I

Getting To Know Cybersecurity

The Evolution of Cybersecurity

Over the past few decades, the idea of cybersecurity has changed dramatically due to the speed at which technology is developing and our growing reliance on digital systems. Cybersecurity has its roots in the early years of computing, specifically in the 1960s and 1970s, when protecting the massive mainframe computers utilized by academic and governmental organizations was the main priority. The concept of computer security during this time was primarily focused on access control and physical security for these devices.

New difficulties surfaced as computer networks started to grow, most notably with the launch of the ARPANET, the forerunner of the current Internet. Although the original purpose of the ARPANET was to enable communication between government agencies and research institutes, it also revealed weaknesses in network security. One of the first common computer worms to impact the ARPANET, the well-known Morris Worm from 1988, brought attention to the necessity of more effective security measures in networked contexts.

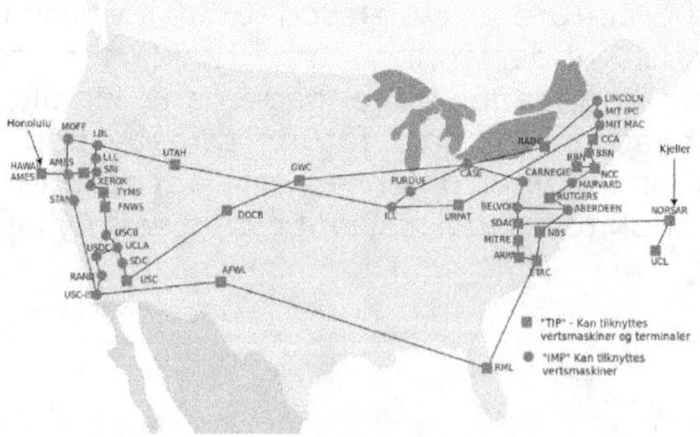

Cybersecurity became a common practice with the introduction of personal computers in the 1980s and the Internet's following development in the 1990s. As more individuals and companies linked to the Internet, the likelihood of cyberattacks rose sharply. In addition to bringing new dangers like malware, viruses, and hacking, the commercialization of the Internet led to the creation of firewalls and antivirus programs to safeguard individuals and businesses.

Numerous significant turning points have formed the area of cybersecurity and impacted its current position.

CFAA, or the Computer Fraud and Abuse Act of 1986. By making unauthorized computer access a federal crime, this U.S. Act demonstrated the government's awareness of cyber threats and the need for legislative frameworks to combat them.

The 1988 film Morris Worm. This event served as a warning to the cybersecurity community. About 10% of the computers online were infected by the Morris Worm, which significantly disrupted operations and exposed the weaknesses in networked systems.

CERT's Establishment (1988). The Defense Advanced Research Projects Agency (DARPA) created the Computer Emergency Response Team (CERT) in reaction to the Morris Worm to handle new computer security issues and offer prompt assistance for security events.

Public Key Cryptography: Its Development (1976). This revolutionary invention, Whitfield Diffie and Martin Hellman first presented, made it possible to communicate securely over unreliable channels and served as the model for numerous contemporary encryption schemes.

The SSL Launch (1994). An essential development for online banking and e-commerce, Netscape created the

Secure Sockets Layer (SSL) protocol to guarantee secure transactions over the Internet.

The ISO/IEC 27001 standard was established in 2005. In addition to encouraging best practices in information security management, this worldwide standard offered a framework for handling and safeguarding sensitive data.

The European Union's General Data Protection Regulation (GDPR) established a new benchmark for privacy and data protection, impacting cybersecurity procedures worldwide and increasing consciousness regarding protecting personal data.

Cybersecurity has become increasingly crucial as we continue to advance in the digital era. The increasing number of internet-connected gadgets has produced a large and intricate digital ecosystem open to cyberattacks, from smartphones to smart home automation systems. The reasons why cybersecurity is more important than ever are as follows:

The sophistication, frequency, and impact of cyberattacks have all increased dramatically. Hacktivists, cybercriminals, and state-sponsored actors employ cutting-edge tactics to compromise networks, steal confidential information, and interfere with services. High-profile events highlight the potential harm and far-reaching effects of cyberattacks, such as the WannaCry ransomware assault in 2017 and the SolarWinds supply chain breach in 2020.

Cybercrime costs the world economy billions of dollars annually, which has a significant negative economic impact. Companies that experience data breaches incur both direct and indirect costs. Direct costs include legal fees, regulatory fines, and remediation expenses. Indirect costs include harm to the company's brand and diminished customer trust.

Digital systems are significant in several vital infrastructure sectors, including transportation, energy, and healthcare. Public safety and national security might suffer significantly from a successful cyberattack on these industries. These systems are becoming increasingly interconnected through the Internet of Things (IoT), making them even more vulnerable.

Organizations gather, store, and process a vast quantity of personal data; thus, protecting and maintaining the privacy of this data is crucial. Regulations such as the California Consumer Privacy Act (CCPA) and the General Data Protection Regulation (GDPR) reflect the growing significance of data protection and the requirement that businesses have robust cybersecurity systems.

While they provide new hazards, emerging technologies like blockchain, AI, and machine learning also present new potential to improve cybersecurity. Attackers can utilize AI and machine learning to construct more complex attacks, but the same technologies can detect and respond to threats more successfully.

The COVID-19 pandemic hastened the digital transformation and remote work adoption trends, increasing the attack surface area for cyber threats. Companies immediately modified their security plans to safeguard cloud-based services and remote workers.

Cybersecurity is an international problem that calls for collaboration between nations. Governments, businesses, and academia must work together to exchange knowledge, establish best practices, and forge a cohesive strategy to counter cyber threats.

The ongoing development of technology and the growing complexity of cyber threats have propelled cybersecurity progress. Cybersecurity has become essential to everyday life, from its early roots in protecting mainframe computers to the contemporary digital era marked by networked devices and sophisticated cyberattacks.

Significant laws, cybersecurity standards, and the creation of public key cryptography are just a few of the critical turning points that have shaped the sector and laid the groundwork for modern procedures. On the other hand, as the digital era advances, cybersecurity becomes increasingly crucial. Strong cybersecurity measures are essential given the rising frequency and sophistication of cyberattacks, the financial damage caused by cybercrime, the need to safeguard personal data and vital infrastructure, and the quick uptake of new technology.

Organizations must be proactive and watchful in this changing environment in their cybersecurity efforts. They should use the newest technologies, follow best practices, and promote a security-aware culture. By doing this, we can guarantee a safer, more secure digital future and better protect the digital frontier.

Defining Cybersecurity

The broad discipline of cybersecurity is devoted to preventing harmful assaults, damage, and unauthorized access from occurring against digital systems, networks, and data. The importance of cybersecurity has increased dramatically as society's reliance on digital infrastructure grows. Navigating this complicated sector requires an understanding of cybersecurity's fundamental terms and concepts and an appreciation of its broad use in today's interconnected world.

Protecting computers, servers, mobile devices, electronic systems, networks, and data from hostile attacks is the fundamental component of cybersecurity. This protection is essential because cyber threats are becoming more frequent and sophisticated. Cybercriminals, from lone hackers to state-sponsored organizations, are constantly developing new ways to exploit holes in digital systems. By using a combination of best practices, procedures, and technologies, cybersecurity seeks to reduce these risks.

The idea of the "threat landscape," which refers to the different kinds of threats that can take advantage of weaknesses in a system, is crucial to cybersecurity. Common dangers include Distributed Denial of Service (DDoS) attacks, which overload a system with traffic to the point of rendering it unusable; phishing attacks, which are false attempts to get sensitive information; and malware, which is harmful software such as viruses, worms, and ransomware. Creating successful defense strategies requires an understanding of the threat landscape.

Another crucial word is "vulnerability," which describes a system's flaw that a threat could exploit. Software, hardware, organizational procedures, and human resources can all have vulnerabilities. Patch management is crucial for reducing these risks since it entails routinely upgrading software to address vulnerabilities. Vulnerabilities are closely associated with "exploits," which are particular methods attackers employ to exploit these flaws.

In cybersecurity, "risk" refers to the possibility of losing money or suffering harm when a threat takes advantage of a weakness. Identifying, evaluating, and prioritizing risks are the first steps in risk management. Next, resources are applied to reduce and manage the likelihood or impact of unfavorable events. To safeguard their most important assets and allocate cybersecurity resources efficiently, organizations must follow this procedure.

One of the fundamental technologies of cybersecurity is encryption, which offers a way to safeguard data by transforming it into a code that stops unwanted access.

Developed in the 1970s, public key encryption is the basis for many contemporary security protocols and enables secure communication via unreliable channels. Data encryption ensures that it cannot be decrypted without the correct decryption key, even if it is intercepted.

In cybersecurity, "authorization" and "authentication" are two crucial steps. Authentication is the process of confirming the identity of a system or user, usually by using multi-factor authentication, biometrics, or passwords. Authorization controls resource access and guarantees that only those with the appropriate permissions may carry out specific tasks. It establishes the range of actions a verified user or system can take.

An essential component of cybersecurity is "incidence response," which describes the steps to control and lessen the effects of a security breach or cyberattack. When a security issue happens, an organization should follow specific procedures, which include detection, containment, eradication, recovery, and lessons learned. These procedures are outlined in an incident response plan. An attack's harm can be significantly minimized, and future occurrences can be avoided with an efficient incident response process.

"Network security," another aspect of cybersecurity, entails safeguarding the availability, integrity, and confidentiality of data while it is transferred over or across networks. This entails putting firewalls, intrusion detection systems, and encryption mechanisms into place to prevent unwanted access and guarantee data privacy. Protecting the data that travels across the internet and between devices and systems within an enterprise is made possible by network security.

Today, cybersecurity covers a broad spectrum of technologies and industries, going well beyond typical IT contexts. Cybersecurity has to consider the unique risks of linked devices, such as industrial control systems and smart home systems, as the Internet of Things (IoT) grows in popularity. IoT devices are appealing targets for attackers because they frequently lack strong security protections. It takes a complete strategy that combines secure design, frequent upgrades, and efficient network segmentation to ensure the security of these devices.

Although cloud computing has completely changed how businesses maintain their IT infrastructure, there are also new security risks. Cloud security includes safeguarding data and apps stored on cloud servers, monitoring cloud providers' compliance with security best practices, and overseeing the shared responsibility model, which assigns separate security tasks to the cloud provider and the client. Identity and access control, data encryption, and ongoing monitoring are all sensible approaches to cloud security.

Cybersecurity is also crucial in the critical infrastructure sector, encompassing energy, transportation, healthcare, and finance. Cyberattacks on vital infrastructure can have disastrous effects, stopping vital services and even putting people in danger. A robust cybersecurity architecture that combines threat intelligence, incident response skills, and cooperation between the public and private sectors is necessary to safeguard vital infrastructure.

Today's cybersecurity also highlights how crucial data protection and regulatory compliance are. Strict guidelines for safeguarding personal information and maintaining privacy are established by laws and regulations like the California Consumer Privacy Act (CCPA) and the General Data Protection Regulation (GDPR) in the European Union. Adherence to these regulations safeguards persons' privacy rights while fostering confidence among stakeholders and customers.

The COVID-19 epidemic has expedited the rise of remote labor, which has broadened the scope of cybersecurity.

Securing remote work settings is essential since employees access company networks and data from various devices and places. This entails setting up virtual private networks (VPNs), deploying secure remote access solutions, and encouraging staff members to practice intense passwords and be on the lookout for phishing scams.

Besides the technological and operational facets, cultivating a security-aware culture within enterprises is another critical aspect of cybersecurity. Employees might unintentionally create security breaches by using weak passwords or clicking on harmful links, making them the weakest link in the cybersecurity chain. Frequent training and awareness initiatives can improve the organization's overall security posture by assisting staff in identifying and averting possible security risks.

The world of cybersecurity is dynamic and fast-changing, constantly adjusting to new threats and technological developments. One cannot stress the significance of taking a proactive and all-encompassing strategy for cybersecurity in light of the growing sophistication of cyber-attacks. This entails putting in place technological controls and best practices, keeping up with new developments in the security and industry sectors, encouraging cross-sector collaboration, and constantly enhancing security measures to guard against ever-changing threats.

In summary, comprehending various fundamental ideas and terminologies, such as threats, vulnerabilities, encryption, and incident response, is necessary to define cybersecurity. Cybersecurity covers many platforms today, including cloud settings, IoT devices, traditional IT systems, critical infrastructure, and remote work configurations. Strong cybersecurity measures are essential to protect our digital lives and uphold our data and systems' availability, integrity, and confidentiality as our reliance on digital technologies grows.

Current Cybersecurity Landscape

Today's complex threats and changing trends in cybersecurity pose a challenge to people, companies, and governments across the globe. It is more crucial than ever to comprehend these risks and the significant actors engaged in thwarting them as digital transformation quickens and technology permeates every part of daily life.

Ransomware is one of the most common threats in today's cybersecurity environment. Malicious software used in ransomware attacks encrypts the victim's data, making it unreadable until a ransom is paid. Attacks of this kind have dramatically increased, primarily aimed at major corporations, healthcare systems, and essential infrastructure. Ransomware can be highly destructive, as seen by the iconic WannaCry attack in 2017 that damaged hundreds of thousands of machines worldwide and the more recent Colonial Pipeline incident in 2021 that disrupted fuel supply in the United States.

Phishing is still a severe danger since it takes advantage of people's weaknesses by sending false emails and messages that lead recipients to install malware or divulge private information. While phishing strategies are widely known, attacks like spear-phishing—targeting particular people or organizations with highly tailored messages—remain prevalent and use ever-more sophisticated techniques. Phishing efforts sometimes rely on social engineering, which takes advantage of people's trust and manipulates their behavior to obtain unauthorized access.

A particularly pernicious type of cyber threat is an Advanced Persistent Threat (APT), characterized by targeted, prolonged attacks usually carried out by highly organized criminal groups or nation-state actors. APTs seek to get into networks and stay there for a long time to provide attackers with the ability to steal confidential information, acquire intelligence, or interfere with regular business activities. The 2020 SolarWinds attack, ascribed to a highly skilled APT cell, exposed several important U.S. government organizations and enterprises, highlighting the grave consequences of these attacks on national security.

New trends are constantly influencing the landscape of cybersecurity in addition to these main concerns. One noteworthy development is the growing use of machine learning (ML) and artificial intelligence (AI) by both attackers and defenders. While cybersecurity experts utilize AI and ML to improve threat detection, response times, and predictive analytics, cybercriminals employ similar technologies to automate and enhance their attacks, producing more flexible and efficient malware.

The Internet of Things (IoT) is increasingly challenging the cybersecurity landscape. The potential attack surface increases with the number of linked devices, giving hackers additional entry points. IoT devices are susceptible to abuse because they frequently lack strong security safeguards. The significant concerns tied to the rise of insecure connected devices were brought to light by the 2016 Mirai botnet assault, which used IoT devices to execute a massive DDoS attack.

The emergence of cloud computing has changed the landscape of information technology by providing flexible and scalable resources but also raising new security issues. Addressing problems like data breaches and misconfigurations and ensuring regulatory standards are followed are necessary for securing cloud infrastructures.

All parties involved in cloud security must thoroughly grasp and diligently implement security measures due to the shared responsibility model, which assigns different security roles to the cloud provider and the client.

The growing regulatory emphasis on privacy and data protection is another significant trend. Strict guidelines for collecting, storing, and processing personal data are established by laws like the California Consumer Privacy Act (CCPA) in the United States and the General Data Protection Regulation (GDPR) in Europe. In addition to defending people's right to privacy, adhering to these requirements requires businesses to implement robust cybersecurity procedures to protect confidential data.

In addition, the involvement of numerous vital actors and stakeholders who collaborate to address these challenges characterizes the cybersecurity landscape. Governments are essential in establishing cybersecurity laws, enforcing rules, and reacting to threats to national security. Organizations that coordinate efforts to safeguard critical infrastructure and offer advice on best practices are the European Union Agency for Cybersecurity (ENISA) and the United States Cybersecurity and Infrastructure Security Agency (CISA).

The Federal Bureau of Investigation (FBI) and INTERPOL, among other law enforcement organizations, are essential in preventing cybercrime, carrying out investigations, and apprehending those responsible. These organizations frequently work together internationally because they understand that cyber dangers are a worldwide problem and call for global cooperation.

Companies in the private sector are the first to defend against cyber-attacks, especially those in the technology and cybersecurity sectors. Businesses like Microsoft, Google, and IBM invest significantly in cybersecurity R&D, developing cutting-edge defenses against dynamic threats. Vendors of cybersecurity products and services, such as Palo Alto Networks, CrowdStrike, and Symantec, offer necessary equipment and services such as firewalls, endpoint security, and threat intelligence.

Furthermore, industry associations and standards organizations are essential for advancing cybersecurity procedures. Enterprises that create standards and guidelines to assist enterprises in implementing efficient security measures and strengthening their cybersecurity posture include the National Institute of Standards and Technology (NIST) and the International Organization for Standardization (ISO). For instance, the NIST Cybersecurity Framework is extensively used in many industries to control and reduce cybersecurity threats.

Academic institutions and non-governmental organizations (NGOs) contribute to the cybersecurity landscape through lobbying, teaching, and research. While NGOs lobby for regulations improving digital security and privacy and increasing awareness about cybersecurity challenges, universities conduct cutting-edge research on cybersecurity technology and threats.

Individuals play a crucial role in the cybersecurity ecosystem. All internet users, including customers and staff, are responsible for ensuring security. Understanding and practicing good cyber hygiene, identifying and responding to threats, and appreciating the value of safeguarding individual and corporate data are all made possible by cybersecurity awareness and education.

In summary, a wide range of significant risks, new developments, and interested parties make up today's dynamic and complicated cybersecurity environment. APTs, phishing, and ransomware present serious obstacles, and the threat landscape is constantly changing due to technologies like cloud computing, AI, and IoT. To protect against cyber threats and advance a safe digital future, governments, law enforcement, private sector businesses, industry consortiums, NGOs, academic institutions, and individuals all play critical responsibilities. The joint efforts of all parties are crucial to protecting our data and upholding confidence in our globalized society as the digital world develops.

CHAPTER II

Emerging Threats and Vulnerabilities

New Threat Vectors

New threat vectors always develop in the quickly changing cybersecurity world, presenting serious difficulties to individuals and companies. The most potent concerns are the development of ransomware, advanced persistent threats (APTs), and sophisticated phishing and social engineering techniques. Remaining secure in an increasingly digital world requires understanding these dangers and the development of effective counterstrategies.

Advanced Persistent Threats (APTs) are highly sophisticated and focused cyberattacks, usually by professional and well-funded attackers. APTs are distinguished from typical cyberattacks by their persistence and long-term goals, which frequently entail espionage, data theft, or the destruction of vital infrastructure. Typical cyberattacks aim to obtain instant financial advantage. APTs typically target particular companies or industries, including financial institutions, defense contractors, government agencies, and suppliers of vital infrastructure.

APTs usually use a multi-phase strategy to enter a target network and establish a foothold. Reconnaissance is frequently used in the first step to find weaknesses and learn more about the target. An initial compromise occurs next, often due to spear-phishing emails or unpatched vulnerability exploits. Once within the network, the attackers use malware and backdoors to create a lasting presence that allows them to move laterally and elevate their rights.

The trickiness of APTs is in their capacity to go unnoticed for long periods—months or even years. Attackers employ cutting-edge strategies, including obfuscation, encryption, and bespoke malware, to avoid being discovered by conventional security measures. They are challenging to detect and eliminate because they constantly modify their strategies in reaction to the target's protective measures. Because APTs are long-lasting, they can cause great harm, from the theft of private data to the interruption of essential services.

Multi-layered security is necessary to reduce the risk of APTs. This entails putting sophisticated threat detection and response tools in place, keeping a close eye on network activities and conducting frequent security audits. Organizations must also prioritize patch management and vulnerability remediation to block possible entry points. In addition, it is imperative to cultivate a cybersecurity-aware culture within the workforce to lower the likelihood of an initial breach via social engineering techniques.

Over the past ten years, ransomware has changed dramatically, emerging as one of the most common and destructive types of cybercrime. The first ransomware attacks were relatively straightforward; they encrypt the victim's data and demand payment in exchange for decryption. On the other hand, modern ransomware varieties are significantly more sophisticated, using double extortion, covert dissemination, and sophisticated encryption algorithms.

A noteworthy development in ransomware is the move toward focused assaults against valuable targets, like as businesses, governmental organizations, and medical facilities. These raids, sometimes called "big-game hunting," entail thorough research to locate vital infrastructure and valuable assets. After that, to maximize the damage and raise the possibility of a ransom payment, attackers use ransomware to encrypt not just the victim's data but also their backups and vital infrastructure.

The use of double extortion is a notable breakthrough in ransomware techniques. Attackers encrypt data, steal confidential data, and threaten to make it public if the ransom is not paid. This strategy increases the pressure on victims because there could be severe legal and reputational repercussions from a data breach. To disclose stolen data, some ransomware gangs have even created specialized leak sites, raising the higher stakes for victims.

Even less technically proficient criminals can now conduct assaults thanks to the emergence of ransomware-as-a-service (RaaS), which has also democratized access to ransomware tools. In return for a portion of the ransom money, RaaS operators give affiliates infrastructure and ransomware kits. Because more players can now engage in this profitable kind of cybercrime, ransomware attacks have increased in frequency due to this approach.

A complete strategy that incorporates strong data protection measures, such as frequent backups, network segmentation, and the deployment of cutting-edge endpoint protection products, is needed to combat ransomware. Organizations must implement efficient incident response protocols to identify and remove ransomware infestations swiftly. Preventing ransomware infestations also requires teaching staff members to spot phishing scams and other attack vectors and cultivating a culture of cybersecurity awareness.

Cybercriminals continue to use phishing and social engineering as two of the most popular and efficient techniques to obtain unauthorized access to systems and data. These strategies make it more difficult to counter since they take advantage of psychological flaws in people rather than technological ones.

Phishing attacks usually entail sending bogus emails from reliable sources, such as banks, coworkers, or respectable businesses. Malicious attachments or links to phony websites intended to steal login information or install malware are frequently seen in these emails. Spear phishing is a highly focused type that increases its chances of success by directing misleading communications toward particular people or companies.

Social engineering techniques encompass more than just phishing emails; they can involve other types of deceit and manipulation. Via social cues and psychological manipulation, attackers can pose as reliable people over the phone or in person and coerce victims into disclosing personal information or taking acts that jeopardize security. Strategies like baiting, pretexting, and quid pro quo frequently exploit people's curiosity and trust.

The proliferation of business email compromise (BEC) methods is a prime example of the growing sophistication of phishing and social engineering attacks. Cybercriminals pose as CEOs or other reliable individuals from an organization in BEC attacks to fool staff members into sending money or divulging private information. In-depth investigation and social engineering are frequently used in these assaults to create persuasive messages to get past conventional email security protocols.

Technology advancements and user education are needed to combat social engineering and phishing. Although they are not infallible, email filtering and anti-phishing technology can aid in thwarting many phishing efforts. To guard against credential theft, organizations must also have strong authentication measures in place, such as multi-factor authentication (MFA). Employees must receive regular security awareness training to be informed on the most recent phishing and social engineering strategies. This will enable them to spot suspicious activity and take the proper action.

In summary, emerging threat vectors, including Advanced Persistent Threats (APTs), sophisticated ransomware, and sophisticated phishing and social engineering techniques, present severe problems in the constantly changing cybersecurity threat landscape. Customized tactics and a multi-layered security approach are needed to counter these threats. Organizations can enhance their cybersecurity by comprehending the characteristics of these threats and putting in place all-encompassing defensive measures to fend off the constantly expanding diversity of cyberattacks. Strong security in an increasingly digital world requires constant attention to detail, flexibility, and education.

Vulnerabilities in Modern Systems

The speed at which technology is developing in the digital age has increased the complexity and sophistication of contemporary systems. Despite being incredibly strong and efficient, these systems are becoming increasingly susceptible to various dangers. It is essential to comprehend the nature of these vulnerabilities to create robust security methods. This section examines the three main types of vulnerabilities in contemporary systems: those caused by human factors, such as insider threats, software, and hardware.

Software vulnerabilities are defects or holes in software that an attacker could use to carry out illegal activities. These vulnerabilities are frequently caused by coding mistakes in the software, insufficient testing, or bad design choices. Buffer overflows, in which an application sends more data to a buffer than it can handle, are typical software vulnerabilities that can result in arbitrary code execution. SQL injection is another common problem in which malevolent actors alter SQL queries to gain unauthorized access to or alter database contents.

These vulnerabilities have been made worse by software programs' growing complexity. Extensive libraries and frameworks, each having possible problems, are frequently used in modern software. Furthermore, because modern systems are interconnected, a vulnerability in one program may impact other applications. The broad adoption of open-source software has also brought about a paradox. Whereas vulnerabilities are publicly known and can be exploited if they are not quickly fixed, open-source software also benefits from community scrutiny and contributions.

Software vulnerabilities usually have a lifetime of discovery, disclosure, and remediation. Security researchers and ethical hackers are essential in locating and disclosing vulnerabilities. But there's usually a delay between a vulnerability being found and patches being released, which leaves systems vulnerable. Cybercriminals frequently take advantage of this exposure window, emphasizing the necessity of automated patch management systems and quick response methods.

Unlike software vulnerabilities, hardware vulnerabilities originate from a system's physical components. These vulnerabilities may result from intentional backdoors during production, manufacturing errors, or design problems. The discovery of the Spectre and Meltdown vulnerabilities in contemporary processors highlighted the severe significance of hardware vulnerabilities. Due to these defects in the architecture of many CPUs, attackers could breach conventional security barriers and access sensitive data from various programs and even virtual machines.

Since hardware is the basis for software operation, hardware vulnerabilities have a significant impact. Resolving hardware vulnerabilities is more complex by nature than resolving software problems. Software updates may be applied rapidly, but fixing hardware defects frequently necessitates a thorough redesign or physical replacement, which is expensive and time-consuming. Furthermore, because hardware components have a lengthy lifespan, vulnerabilities may remain undiscovered for many years, making thorough remediation challenging.

The supply chain is another facet of hardware vulnerabilities. As manufacturing has become more globalized, parts are frequently obtained from several suppliers in various geographical locations. The possibility of manipulated components entering the supply chain due to either evil intent or inadequate quality control is increased by this diversification. Thorough testing procedures and strict supply chain management techniques are needed to guarantee the integrity of hardware components.

Although technological vulnerabilities are frequently the focus of attention, human factors remain an essential and often overlooked aspect of system security. Human factors include everything from straightforward user error to sophisticated social engineering attacks. Phishing is a classic example of an assault that takes advantage of human weaknesses when perpetrators trick victims into disclosing private information. Despite improvements in user education and email filtering, phishing is still one of the most potent attack methods.

A particularly pernicious kind of human vulnerability is insider threats. Because of their insider status and expertise, insiders have the potential to harm an organization through intentional or unintentional activities seriously. Insiders with malicious intent may steal intellectual property, disrupt systems, or divulge private information. Conversely, unintended insiders may become targets of social engineering schemes or unintentionally alter vital system configurations, which could result in security lapses.

Insider threats can have many reasons, ranging from coercion and ideological views to financial gain and personal grudges. Identifying and mitigating insider threats can be challenging because doing so necessitates differentiating between trusted employees' typical and unusual conduct. The necessity to strike a balance between privacy and security measures, as well as the possible effects on employee morale, complicates this work. Insider threat indicators can be found through behavior patterns that are increasingly detected by advanced analytics and machine learning. However, these techniques could be better and must be adjusted carefully to prevent false positives.

Modern system vulnerabilities necessitate a multipronged strategy incorporating process enhancements, technology fixes, and human-centered tactics. Best practices for software vulnerabilities include strict testing, secure coding guidelines, and automated tools for patch management and vulnerability detection. Frequent penetration tests and security audits can assist in finding vulnerabilities and addressing them before they are used against you.

Supply chain management, extensive testing, and secure design principles are required to address hardware vulnerabilities. Organizations should collaborate closely with hardware providers to ensure that hardware components fulfill security requirements and are free of known vulnerabilities. Organizations must be ready to apply mitigations such as microcode updates or, in the worst situations, hardware replacements if hardware vulnerabilities are found after deployment.

Education, knowledge, and culture must be prioritized in light of human aspects and insider threats. Frequent training sessions can assist staff members in identifying and handling social engineering and phishing efforts. Essential components of a thorough security strategy include putting in place strong access controls, keeping an eye on user behavior, and creating a culture where staff members feel comfortable reporting suspicious conduct.

In summary, modern systems have many different types of vulnerabilities, including hardware, software, and human factors. Every kind of vulnerability has different difficulties and needs a different mitigating strategy. Organizations may strengthen their ability to safeguard systems and data in an ever-evolving threat landscape by identifying and mitigating these vulnerabilities via technology innovations, process optimizations, and human-centered approaches. These measures must be integrated with constant attention and adaptability to maintain strong security in the face of changing threats.

Case Studies of Recent Cyber Attacks

Cyber-attacks have gotten more complex in the digital age, disrupting businesses worldwide and costing them a lot of money. Examining previous cyberattacks offers essential insights into the strategies used by attackers and the weaknesses they take advantage of. By understanding these situations, organizations can strengthen and better prepare their defenses against future threats. This section looks at three prominent case studies of recent cyberattacks, evaluating the security breaches and drawing meaningful conclusions.

The SolarWinds attack, detected in December 2020, was one of the most significant cyberattacks in recent memory. To carry out this intricate supply chain attack, malicious malware had to be introduced into SolarWinds' popular IT management program, Orion. Approximately 18,000 users, including several government organizations and Fortune 500 companies, received the corrupted software upgrades.

The assailants thought to be connected to a nation-state, concealed themselves and avoided capture by employing cutting-edge strategies. By creating a backdoor into the compromised systems, the SUNBURST malware allowed the attackers to steal confidential information and travel laterally across networks. The attackers had full access to the victims' networks for several months while the breach went unnoticed.

The SolarWinds attack brought to light several vital lessons. It first emphasized how crucial supply chain security is. Companies need to ensure that third-party software complies with strict security standards and thoroughly screens their vendors. Second, the attack illustrated the necessity of solid detection and monitoring tools. To quickly discover and address unusual activity, advanced threat detection techniques and ongoing network monitoring are necessary. Finally, the hack highlighted how critical it is to implement a zero-trust architecture in which every access request—regardless of where it comes from—is carefully examined.

One of the biggest fuel pipeline operators in the US, Colonial Pipeline, was attacked with ransomware in May

2021. After breaking into the company's IT network, the Dark Side ransomware group encrypted important data and demanded a fee to unlock it. Due to the attack, Colonial Pipeline was forced to cease operations, which resulted in significant gasoline shortages and panic purchasing throughout the eastern part of the US.

A virtual private network (VPN) account password that was hacked gave the attackers first access to Colonial Pipeline's network. This event made multi-factor authentication (MFA) and strong password policies critical. The attacker's ability to exploit a single point of failure due to the absence of multi-factor authentication highlights the need for layered security protections.

Critical infrastructure vulnerabilities were also made public with the Colonial Pipeline hack. The closure significantly impacted society and the economy, highlighting how crucial it is to protect vital services. To lessen the effect of any attacks, organizations in charge of critical infrastructure must prioritize cybersecurity investments, carry out frequent vulnerability assessments, and create robust incident response plans.

The incident also brought attention to the problem of ransom payments. To hasten the rebuilding of their systems, Colonial Pipeline sent the attackers over $4.4 million in cryptocurrencies. Even though the choice was made to resume operations promptly, it highlighted the moral and tactical issues organizations must deal with while handling ransomware. Ransom payments may not ensure complete data recovery and may encourage additional criminal activity. Therefore, Organizations must consider the possible outcomes and look into other options, such as keeping thorough backups and creating robust recovery plans.

Microsoft Exchange Server was the victim of a massive cyberattack at the beginning of 2021 linked to the state-sponsored Hafnium organization. By taking advantage of several Exchange Server zero-day vulnerabilities, the attackers could access email accounts without authorization and set up backdoors for additional exploitation. The attack impacted tens of thousands of organizations globally, including corporations, governmental bodies, and educational institutions.

The Microsoft Exchange Server attack highlighted how crucial timely patch management is. To fix the vulnerabilities, Microsoft provided security upgrades. However, many firms still need to install them, leaving their systems vulnerable. This incident made it clear that to reduce the danger of exploitation, organizations must prioritize quickly implementing security patches.

The attack also highlighted the difficulties in identifying and addressing zero-day vulnerabilities. To obtain initial access and build persistence within targeted networks, advanced threat actors frequently use these undiscovered vulnerabilities. Organizations must invest in endpoint detection and response (EDR) systems and threat intelligence to quickly identify and address such threats.

The extensive effects of the Microsoft Exchange Server attack underscored enterprises' need for a defense-in-depth strategy. In today's threat world, more than perimeter protection is required. Network segmentation, robust authentication procedures, and frequent security audits are examples of multi-layered security controls that can be implemented to reduce the impact of a compromise and stop lateral network movement.

Enterprises can implement several recurring themes and takeaways from the analysis of these case studies to improve their cybersecurity posture. Organizations should put a proactive approach to security first and foremost. This entails doing frequent vulnerability scans, penetration tests, and risk assessments to find and fix potential vulnerabilities before they can be used against you.

Secondly, robust incident response plans are necessary to reduce the impact of cyberattacks. To ensure that all parties involved are aware of their roles and duties during an event, organizations should design and test their response protocols regularly. Establishing internal and external communication channels is part of coordinating reaction activities and giving affected parties timely updates.

Thirdly, training programs and cybersecurity awareness are essential for reducing risks associated with people. Workers should receive training on safe computer procedures, social engineering strategies, and recent phishing techniques. Establishing a cybersecurity awareness culture can help firms lower the probability of successful attacks resulting from carelessness or human mistakes.

Additionally, to defend against various threats, organizations need to implement a layered security approach incorporating numerous protections. This entails implementing robust access controls like encryption, network segmentation, and multi-factor authentication. Real-time threat identification and mitigation depend on sophisticated threat detection and response capabilities, ongoing monitoring, and logging.

To share threat intelligence and best practices, firms should actively interact with peers in the sector, government agencies, and cybersecurity specialists. Since cyber threats are constantly changing, a team approach to security can increase resilience. Organizations can avoid developing dangers by participating in information-sharing programs and keeping up with the latest trends in threats.

In conclusion, recent cyberattacks have highlighted the dynamic nature of cyber threats and the vital need for strong cybersecurity measures. Examples of these attacks include the Microsoft Exchange Server exploit, the ransomware attack on Colonial Pipeline, and the SolarWinds breach. Organizations may improve their readiness and defenses against future assaults by examining these significant breaches and noting the lessons they provide. A robust cybersecurity strategy must include employee awareness, layered security defenses, collaborative efforts within the cybersecurity community, proactive risk management, and thorough incident response plans.

CHAPTER III

Cybersecurity Strategies and Frameworks

Developing a Cybersecurity Strategy

Creating a solid cybersecurity strategy is essential for businesses looking to safeguard their data, keep operations running smoothly, and preserve their brand in an increasingly digital world. Such a strategy must be carefully crafted through careful strategic planning, risk management, and goal and priority setting. By taking a comprehensive approach, companies may build a robust cybersecurity posture by being proactive in their defenses and reactive to attacks.

In cybersecurity, strategic planning entails organizing the organization's security objectives, determining the resources required, and detailing the actions necessary to meet those objectives. It starts with a comprehensive evaluation of cybersecurity today, which includes a look at potential threats, vulnerabilities, and the organization's overall security posture. This first step gives a clear picture of the organization's current state and areas that require improvement.

Aligning cybersecurity measures with the organization's overarching business goals is crucial to strategic planning. This alignment guarantees that, rather than impeding, security measures assist and improve company activities. For example, An organization that prioritizes digital transformation needs to incorporate cybersecurity into all phases of its technical development. Rather than adding security features later, this integration aids in securing new digital projects from the start.

Strategic planning also includes establishing a reasonable timeframe for accomplishing cybersecurity objectives. This timeline should consider short-term goals, like fixing essential vulnerabilities, and long-term goals, like raising cybersecurity awareness inside the company. The strategy plan must be reviewed and adjusted regularly to address the changing threat environment and new technology developments.

The foundation of any successful cybersecurity strategy is risk management. It entails locating, evaluating, and reducing risks that can jeopardize a company's information assets. A risk assessment is the first step in the risk management process; it identifies potential threats, vulnerabilities, and the chance they may materialize. The possible effects of these hazards on the organization are also assessed in this assessment.

After identifying hazards, they need to be ranked according to the likelihood and severity of their occurrence. High-priority risks should be dealt with immediately, mainly if they cause significant financial loss or harm one's reputation. Although they are substantial, lower-priority concerns can be handled over a more extended period.

Next, mitigation plans are created to deal with the hazards that have been identified. These tactics may involve implementing administrative and technical controls, such as policies and processes, intrusion detection systems, and firewalls. For example, a risk related to phishing attempts can be reduced by combining employee training programs with email screening technologies.

Another aspect of risk management is keeping a close eye on the cybersecurity scene for emerging threats and weaknesses. The nature of cyber dangers is ever-changing; thus, it is imperative to maintain this constant attention. Updating risk assessments and mitigation plans guarantees the company is safeguarded against new risks.

Incident response planning constitutes a significant component of risk management. Security events can and do happen even with the finest protective measures. In the event of a security breach, an efficient incident response plan describes what has to be done to limit the issue, lessen its effects, and recover from it. Protocols for communication should be included in this strategy so that regulatory agencies and stakeholders are informed as needed.

A cybersecurity strategy can only be successfully implemented if its goals and priorities are clearly defined. Objectives guide the organization's security goals, while priorities facilitate the effective use of resources by directing them toward the most urgent problems.

Goals should be time-bound, relevant, measurable, achievable, and specific (SMART). One goal is to cut down on the number of successful phishing attempts by half over the following year. This goal is time-bound (within the next year), relevant (phishing is a common threat), quantifiable (a 50% reduction in phishing attacks), and specific (reducing phishing attacks).

Determining which goals are most important to the organization's business operations and security posture is the first step in setting priorities. Based on a risk-based methodology, this prioritizing should be done with an emphasis on first reducing the most significant risks. Updating encryption procedures should be an essential priority, for instance, if a risk assessment indicates that a sizable amount of the organization's sensitive data is in danger owing to antiquated encryption techniques.

When determining priorities, companies should consider industry best practices and regulatory requirements in addition to risk-based prioritizing. Adherence to regulatory frameworks like the General Data Protection Regulation (GDPR) and the Health Insurance Portability and Accountability Act (HIPAA) necessitates the implementation of particular security protocols. Similarly, following industry norms like the NIST Cybersecurity Framework can offer a solid basis for developing an effective cybersecurity plan.

Establishing goals and priorities also requires teamwork and communication. The involvement of multiple stakeholders, including IT, legal, finance, and executive management, guarantees the cybersecurity plan is all-encompassing and in line with the organization's overarching objectives. Regularly informing all parties about advancements and difficulties promotes openness and a shared commitment to accomplishing security goals.

Lastly, establishing priorities and goals should be a process that is repeated. The organization's cybersecurity requirements will alter as it expands and the threat landscape changes. Maintaining the relevance and efficacy of the cybersecurity strategy requires regular reviews and updates of goals and priorities. Using an iterative approach, the business can also benefit from new practices and technology that can improve its security posture.

Creating a solid cybersecurity plan requires thoughtful goal- and priority-setting, thorough risk management, and strategic planning. Strategic planning is an organized method for establishing and accomplishing cybersecurity objectives, whereas risk management recognizes, evaluates, and eliminates possible risks. Establishing well-defined goals and priorities guarantees that resources are distributed effectively, initially prioritizing the most crucial areas. By combining these components, organizations can create a robust cybersecurity posture that supports their goals, safeguards their information assets, and maintains operations in the increasingly digital environment. The cybersecurity strategy must be reviewed and adjusted regularly to keep up with changing threats and sustain strong security over time.

Key Frameworks and Standards

Organizations must implement solid frameworks and standards to protect their information assets, guarantee compliance, and preserve operational integrity when cybersecurity threats constantly change. Two of the most well-known and extensively used frameworks are ISO/IEC 27001 and the NIST Cybersecurity Framework. Comprehensive cybersecurity strategies also benefit from other pertinent standards that provide organized methods for risk management, data protection, and incident response.

Since its introduction in 2014, the National Institute of Standards and Technology (NIST) Cybersecurity Framework has become an essential cybersecurity resource. It was created in response to an executive order meant to strengthen cybersecurity for vital infrastructure in the US. Nonetheless, its applicability transcends national boundaries and industry domains, rendering it an internationally acknowledged benchmark for augmenting corporate cybersecurity.

The five main components of the NIST Cybersecurity Framework are Identify, Protect, Detect, Respond, and Recover. Every function has distinct subcategories and categories that offer in-depth instructions on managing cybersecurity risks.

Identifying entails managing cybersecurity threats to systems, assets, data, and capabilities by comprehending the organization's environment. The corporate environment, governance, risk assessment, and risk management plan are all included in this.

Protect concentrates on measures to guarantee the provision of essential infrastructure services. Key areas include protective technology, maintenance, data security, information protection policies and procedures, awareness and training, and access control.

Detect comprises creating and putting into action plans to find cybersecurity events. This includes security continuous monitoring, mechanisms for detection, and ongoing monitoring to identify anomalies and occurrences.

Respond entails creating and carrying out plans to address a cybersecurity occurrence that has been identified. Planning for responses, communicating, analyzing, mitigating, and improving are all covered in this.

Recover entails upholding resilience strategies and reestablishing any services or capabilities hampered by a cybersecurity incident. Recovery planning, enhancements, and communication are essential areas.

Because of its adaptability, the NIST Framework may be customized for various businesses, regardless of size or sector. Acting as a link between different cybersecurity best practices and standards helps companies match up their current procedures and controls with an all-encompassing, risk-based strategy.

The International Organization for Standardization (ISO) and the International Electrotechnical Commission (IEC) have published ISO/IEC 27001, an international standard for information security management systems (ISMS). It offers a systematic way to handle private company data while guaranteeing its availability, confidentiality, and integrity.

Specific guidelines for creating, putting into practice, upholding, and continuously enhancing an ISMS are provided by ISO/IEC 27001. It takes a risk-based approach to information security, requiring companies to evaluate their risks and implement the necessary controls to lessen them.

There are eleven clauses and fourteen annexed domains in the standard. Organizational Context. Being aware of the stakeholders, the organizational context, and their needs.

Leadership. I am determining roles and duties, creating an information security policy, and securing a commitment from upper management.

Planning. It is identifying opportunities and threats, establishing goals for information security, and organizing how to get there.

Support. The tools, know-how, awareness, dialogue, and recorded data are required to back up the ISMS.

Operation. We are implementing controls and procedures and overseeing them to accomplish information security goals.

Performance Evaluation. Internal audits and management reviews are among the methods used to measure, monitor, analyze, and assess the performance of the ISMS.

Improvement. We are dealing with nonconformities, taking corrective action, and enhancing the ISMS over time.

Asset management, access control, cryptography, physical and environmental security, operations security, communications security, system acquisition, development and maintenance, supplier relationships, incident management, and compliance are just a few information security-related topics covered by the annexed domains.

A company's dedication to information security is demonstrated by its ISO/IEC 27001 accreditation, which also reassures stakeholders that strong security measures are in place. Accredited certification bodies conduct a thorough external audit as part of the certification process to verify that the standards are being followed.

In addition to NIST and ISO/IEC 27001, several other standards that focus on risk management and information security add to an all-encompassing cybersecurity framework.

ISO/IEC 27002. Based on ISO/IEC 27001, this standard offers best practice recommendations for information security measures. It guides when choosing and putting controls in place to satisfy ISMS criteria.

Information and Related Technologies Control Objectives (COBIT). COBIT is a framework for IT governance and management that ISACA created. It offers extensive procedures, policies, and controls to guarantee efficient IT governance and match IT strategy with corporate objectives.

Payment Card Industry Data Security Standard, or **PCI DSS**: This standard aims to safeguard cardholder information and guarantee safe credit card transactions. It outlines particular security requirements and controls and applies to enterprises that handle, store, or transmit credit card information.

General Data Protection Regulation, or GDPR, is a legislative framework. Still, it also imposes strict privacy and data protection standards on enterprises that handle the personal data of EU individuals. It highlights how crucial incident response, risk management, and data security are.

The Center for Internet Security Controls, or CIS Controls. A global group of professionals produced a set of cybersecurity best practices known as the CIS Controls. They give firms practical advice on protecting themselves from frequent cyberattacks, emphasizing crucial topics like hardware and software asset inventory and control, safe setups, and ongoing vulnerability management.

NIST SP 800-53. This standard, which NIST published, offers a list of privacy and security safeguards for federal information systems and organizations. It provides a thorough framework for choosing and defining controls to safeguard people, property, and organizational activities.

Cloud Security Alliance Cloud Controls Matrix, or CSA CCM. This framework offers comprehensive security controls specifically designed for cloud computing settings. Ensuring adherence to industry standards and best practices assists enterprises in evaluating and managing security risks associated with the cloud.

Using these frameworks and standards, firms may manage cybersecurity risks organizationally, ensure regulatory compliance, and improve their security posture. Organizations frequently combine many standards to establish a complete cybersecurity plan covering various information security issues since each standard has distinct advantages.

To sum up, to create a robust cybersecurity plan, it is necessary to use essential frameworks and standards like the ISO/IEC 27001 and NIST Cybersecurity Framework in conjunction with other pertinent standards like COBIT, PCI DSS, GDPR, CIS Controls, NIST SP 800-53, and CSA CCM. These frameworks offer firms organized methods for handling risk, safeguarding data, and responding to incidents, assisting them in navigating the intricate world of cybersecurity. By implementing and integrating these standards, organizations can improve their security posture, guarantee compliance, and protect their vital information assets in an increasingly digital environment. Maintaining strong security over time and staying ahead of evolving cyber threats need constant assessment and adaptation of these standards.

Implementation Best Practices

Implementing cybersecurity frameworks and standards effectively is a complex yet essential task for organizations striving to protect their digital assets. The journey from planning to execution requires a thorough understanding of best practices, practical steps, and strategies to overcome common challenges. Organizations can enhance their security posture and achieve their cybersecurity objectives by following a structured approach.

The first step in implementing a cybersecurity framework is a comprehensive assessment of the current security posture. This involves identifying existing security measures, assessing vulnerabilities, and understanding the specific requirements of the chosen framework. Based on this assessment, a detailed implementation plan should be developed, outlining the scope, objectives, timelines, resources, and responsibilities.

Successful implementation requires the involvement and commitment of various organizational stakeholders, including top management, IT staff, and end-users. Effective communication ensures that everyone understands the importance of the cybersecurity initiatives, their roles, and the expected outcomes. Regular updates and feedback sessions help maintain engagement and promptly address concerns.

Adequate resources, both financial and human, are crucial for the successful implementation of cybersecurity measures. Organizations should allocate sufficient budgets for technology investments, hiring skilled personnel, and conducting training programs. Training is essential as it equips employees with the knowledge and skills to adhere to security policies and practices, reducing human risks.

Developing comprehensive security policies and procedures is a fundamental aspect of cybersecurity implementation. These policies should cover various areas, such as data protection, access control, incident response, and compliance. Clear and well-documented policies ensure consistency and provide a reference point for employees. Regular reviews and updates are necessary to keep these policies relevant and effective.

Implementing the right technology solutions is critical for enhancing cybersecurity. This includes deploying firewalls, intrusion detection systems, encryption tools, endpoint protection, and continuous monitoring solutions. Organizations should prioritize technologies aligning with their risk profiles and business needs. Additionally, integrating these technologies seamlessly into existing systems is essential to avoid disruptions.

A robust risk management process is essential for identifying, assessing, and mitigating cybersecurity risks. Organizations should implement controls that address identified risks and continuously monitor their effectiveness. This includes conducting regular vulnerability assessments, penetration testing, and audits to ensure security measures remain effective against evolving threats.

Developing and testing an incident response plan is crucial for minimizing the impact of security breaches. The plan should outline the steps during an incident, including containment, eradication, recovery, and communication. Regular drills and simulations help prepare the response team and ensure the plan is effective. Additionally, having a recovery strategy in place ensures that critical operations can be restored quickly.

Cybersecurity is an ongoing process that requires continuous improvement. Organizations should regularly review their security measures, assess their performance, and make necessary adjustments. Staying informed about the latest threat trends, technological advancements, and regulatory changes is essential. Compliance with relevant standards and regulations, such as GDPR, HIPAA, and PCI DSS, should be a priority, ensuring that the organization meets legal and industry requirements.

One of the organizations' most common challenges is being insured for more resources, including budget and skilled personnel. To address this, organizations can prioritize their cybersecurity initiatives based on risk assessments, focusing on the most critical areas first. Outsourcing certain security functions to managed security service providers (MSSPs) can also be cost-effective, providing access to specialized expertise without significant in-house investment.

Implementing new cybersecurity measures often requires changes in workflows and behavior, which can meet resistance from employees. Overcoming this challenge requires effective change management strategies, including clear communication about the benefits of the new measures, providing training and support, and involving employees in the process. Leadership should actively endorse and participate in the initiatives to demonstrate their importance.

Integrating new security technologies with existing systems can be complex and may lead to operational disruptions. To mitigate this, organizations should conduct thorough planning and testing before deployment. Selecting interoperable solutions and working closely with vendors and experts can help ensure smooth integration. Additionally, phased implementation can minimize the impact on operations.

The constantly evolving nature of cyber threats poses a significant challenge to maintaining adequate security measures. Organizations should adopt a proactive approach to threat intelligence, staying informed about the latest attack vectors and tactics. Regularly updating security technologies and processes, conducting threat hunting, and participating in information-sharing networks can help organizations avoid potential threats.

Navigating the complex landscape of cybersecurity regulations and standards can be challenging, especially for organizations operating in multiple jurisdictions. To address this, organizations should establish a compliance management program that includes regular audits, gap analysis, and updates to policies and procedures. Engaging legal and compliance experts can provide valuable guidance and ensure adherence to all applicable regulations.

Insider threats, whether malicious or unintentional, can be challenging to detect and mitigate. Implementing stringent access controls, monitoring user activities, and fostering a culture of security awareness are essential steps. Organizations should also conduct regular security training and awareness programs to educate employees about the risks and their role in protecting sensitive information.

Despite the best preventive measures, security incidents can still occur. Many organizations need more preparation and coordination with effective incident responsen.. Developing a detailed incident response plan, conducting regular drills, and ensuring that the response team is well-trained and equipped are critical steps. Learning from past incidents and continuously improving the response process can enhance preparedness.

Reliance on third-party vendors and partners introduces additional security risks. Organizations should implement a robust third-party risk management program that includes thorough due diligence, contractually binding security requirements, and continuous monitoring of third-party activities. Regular assessments and audits of third-party security practices help ensure they meet the organization's standards.

In conclusion, implementing effective cybersecurity frameworks and standards involves a series of practical steps and the ability to navigate everyday challenges. Organizations can build a robust cybersecurity posture by conducting comprehensive assessments, engaging stakeholders, allocating resources, developing policies, deploying technology, managing risks, and preparing for incidents. Overcoming challenges such as resource constraints, resistance to change, technology integration complexities, evolving threats, compliance requirements, insider threats, incident response preparedness, and third-party risks requires strategic planning, continuous improvement, and a proactive approach. Through these efforts, organizations can enhance their resilience against cyber threats and protect their critical information assets.

CHAPTER IV

Advanced Defensive Technologies

Next-Generation Firewalls and Intrusion Detection Systems

The need for sophisticated security measures increases as cyber threats become more complex. Intrusion detection systems (IDS) and next-generation firewalls (NGFWs) are essential in today's cybersecurity infrastructures. They have enhanced threat detection and mitigation capabilities but have various drawbacks and difficulties. Effective implementation techniques are necessary. To fully protect organizational assets and optimize their benefits

Next-generation firewalls incorporate cutting-edge technologies intended to counter modern cyber threats, going beyond the capabilities of classic firewalls. Deep packet inspection (DPI), which allows the firewall to examine data packet contents and header information, is one of the main features of NGFWs. This is made possible by more precise control and the capacity to identify and stop complex threats that conventional firewalls would overlook.

The knowledge and control of applications is another important feature of NGFWs. Conventional firewalls usually concentrate on IP addresses and ports while operating at the network layer. NGFWs, on the other hand, can recognize and manage applications independent of the port or protocol they employ. This functionality is essential in settings where programs employ dynamic ports or port-hopping strategies to avoid detection.

Integrated intrusion prevention systems (IPS) are another feature of NGFWs. NGFWs can identify and stop known vulnerabilities, zero-day attacks, and advanced persistent threats (APTs) by fusing firewall and intrusion prevention system (IPS) capabilities. The security architecture is made simpler by this integration, which also improves threat detection and prevention efficiency.

NGFWs also provide enhanced threat intelligence capabilities. They use real-time threat intelligence streams to remain informed about the most recent trends and indicators of threat activity. This improves the security posture by enabling them to recognize and stop threats based on the most recent data.

Even with their sophisticated powers, NGFWs have many drawbacks. The possibility of performance decrease is one significant restriction. Resource-intensive procedures like deep packet inspection can cause latency and lower network speed, particularly in situations with high traffic. Businesses must know their performance needs and select NGFW solutions that will grow with them.

The complexity of configuration and management is another drawback. For enterprises needing more specialized security knowledge, the abundance of capabilities and customization possibilities NGFWs offers may be daunting. Misconfigurations can lower the firewall's efficacy and result in security holes. To guarantee correct configuration and management, investing in training and outside expertise is imperative.

Furthermore, although NGFWs offer robust security features, they are not a panacea. They can have trouble identifying new or highly complex attacks that don't follow recognizable patterns but are good at stopping established threats and patterns. A more complete defense can be achieved by combining NGFWs with other security measures like behavioral analytics and endpoint detection and response (EDR) programs.

Systems for detecting intrusions are essential for spotting hostile and illegal activity on a network. IDS systems fall into two primary categories: host-based IDS (HIDS) and network-based IDS (NIDS). While HIDS keeps an eye out for indications of compromise on specific host systems, NIDS monitors network traffic for unusual activities.

Among IDS's main features is signature-based detection. This technique makes use of pre-established signs of recognized dangers. The IDS sends an alert when system activity or network traffic coincides with a signature. Signature-based detection is quite effective when it comes to promptly and precisely identifying known threats.

Many intrusion detection systems use anomaly-based detection in addition to signature-based detection. This technique finds departures from the norm by creating a baseline of typical network or system activity. Threats that have never been seen before and zero-day assaults that don't match any signatures can be found using anomaly-based detection.

IDS also offers useful forensic and logging features. IDS systems allow security teams to investigate occurrences, comprehend attack paths, and gather evidence for regulatory compliance or legal action by capturing extensive logs of network and system activities. This skill is necessary for post-event analysis and ongoing security measure enhancement.

IDS has limits even if it provides essential detecting features. The high rate of false positives is one major drawback. In particular, anomaly-based detection can offer many alerts for innocuous behaviors that depart from the predefined baseline. Investigating these notifications requires time and resources from security professionals, which may cause alert fatigue and cause them to miss real threats.

The classic IDS's passive design is another drawback. IDS can identify and notify users of suspicious activity, but it can not proactively block or lessen risks. Organizations must combine intrusion detection systems (IDS) with other security solutions, such as intrusion prevention systems (IPS) or automated response tools, to allow active threat mitigation.

IDS solutions can also require a lot of resources. They need a lot of computing power and storage to analyze and store vast amounts of system logs and network data. Organizations with limited resources or high network traffic may find this especially difficult.

The first stage for NGFWs is to carry out a comprehensive needs assessment. This entails knowing the network design, security requirements, and performance factors. Organizations can choose NGFW solutions that meet their requirements and guarantee they can manage network traffic without experiencing appreciable performance reduction based on the results of this assessment.

Another critical factor is NGFW positioning. To efficiently monitor and manage incoming and outgoing traffic, they should be installed at crucial network intersections, such as those connecting internal networks to external connections. Maintaining the firewall's effectiveness against the most recent threats requires updating the NGFW's firmware and threat intelligence feeds.

The first step in implementing IDS effectively is choosing the right kind for the company's environment. While HIDS is more appropriate for securing individual hosts, NIDS is perfect for monitoring network traffic. The capacity of intrusion detection systems (IDS) to identify suspicious activity is improved by strategically deploying them at crucial network locations, including data centers, vital servers, and network perimeters.

Integrating IDS with other security solutions, such as SIEM (Security Information and Event Management) systems, can enhance incident response capabilities. SIEM systems provide a comprehensive picture of the security landscape and facilitate quicker and more efficient incident response by aggregating and correlating signals from IDS and other sources.

IDS signatures and anomaly detection parameters must be adjusted and updated regularly to lower false positives and preserve detection accuracy. Security teams should periodically evaluate and modify detection criteria in response to new threats and modifications in network behavior.

Critical elements of implementation also include awareness-raising and training. Security staff members need to know the strengths and weaknesses of NGFWs and IDS. It is ensured by ongoing instruction and practical training that they can handle and react to the alarms produced by these systems.

In summary, intrusion detection systems and next-generation firewalls are essential components of contemporary cybersecurity toolsets. They have inherent limits that must be addressed, but they also offer enhanced capabilities for detecting and mitigating a wide range of threats. Organizations can improve their security posture and safeguard their vital assets from ever-evolving cyber threats by adhering to best practices for deployment, which include comprehensive assessment, strategic placement, frequent updates, integration with other security technologies, and ongoing training.

Endpoint Protection and Response (EPR)

Securing endpoints—devices like laptops, desktop computers, smartphones, and tablets—has become increasingly important as cyber threats change. Cybercriminals frequently use these devices as their primary targets when trying to exploit security holes and access larger network systems. To solve these issues, advanced detection, response, and remediation capabilities are combined in Endpoint Protection and Response (EPR) solutions. Maintaining a strong cybersecurity posture requires understanding the function of Endpoint Detection and Response (EDR) tools and practical endpoint security methods.

Tools for endpoint detection and response, or EDR, are essential to contemporary endpoint security plans. With the help of these technologies, endpoint actions are continuously monitored and analyzed to identify suspicious activity, react quickly to threats, and resolve incidents. EDR solutions improve an organization's endpoint protection by providing several essential features.

The ongoing monitoring and visibility provided by EDR tools is one of its primary purposes. EDR systems continually monitor endpoint activities, recording precise information on processes, network connections, and file changes, unlike typical antivirus solutions that depend on sporadic scans. Security personnel can spot strange activities that can point to a compromise thanks to this real-time visibility.

To identify threats, EDR technologies also use machine learning and advanced analytics. Analyzing large amounts of data, these systems can recognize trends and abnormalities linked to malicious activity. This involves spotting advanced persistent threats (APTs), fileless malware, and zero-day exploits that conventional signature-based detection techniques might overlook. Based on past data, machine learning models predict possible attacks and discover subtle indicators of compromise (IOCs).

Incident response and remediation are vital features of EDR technologies. EDR solutions offer automated or guided reaction steps, like isolating infected endpoints, stopping harmful processes, and uninstalling malware when a threat is recognized. This capacity to respond quickly is essential for reducing the effect of security events and preventing attackers from moving laterally throughout the network.

Strong forensic capabilities are another benefit of EDR systems. They help security teams investigate security incidents in depth by keeping a historical record of endpoint actions. This entails determining the attack's primary cause, comprehending its vector, and estimating the scope of the compromise. By learning from previous attacks, forensic analysis assists organizations in strengthening their defenses and averting more incidents.

Effective endpoint security solutions must be implemented using a blend of corporate policies, best practices, and technology safeguards. Organizations can lower the risk of successful cyberattacks and improve endpoint security using a holistic approach.

Implementing strong access controls is one of the fundamental techniques for endpoint security. This involves confirming the identity of users gaining access to endpoint devices by implementing robust authentication methods like multi-factor authentication (MFA). By forcing users to give several kinds of authentication, MFA adds an extra layer of security, making it more difficult for attackers to obtain illegal access.

Endpoint encryption is an additional necessary precaution. Data stored on endpoints can be safeguarded and rendered unreadable to unauthorized users using encryption, even if a device is lost or stolen. Often used techniques to prevent access to sensitive data are file-level encryption and full disk encryption.

Patch management and routine software updates shield endpoints from known vulnerabilities. It is recommended that organizations implement a systematic procedure for updating and patching operating systems, apps, and firmware with security fixes. By doing this, security holes that an attacker could exploit are closed, and endpoints are kept safe from new threats.

Implementing endpoint protection platforms (EPP), which fuse sophisticated threat detection tools with conventional antivirus software, is also critical. With its multi-layered approach to endpoint security, EPP solutions offer defense against various threats, including ransomware, malware, and phishing attempts. These platforms employ real-time threat intelligence, behavior monitoring, and heuristic analysis to identify and stop harmful activity.

Another helpful tactic for protecting endpoints is network segmentation. Organizations can lessen the possible impact of a compromised endpoint by segmenting the network into smaller parts and limiting connectivity between them. As a result, hackers cannot move laterally across the network and get access to private or sensitive systems.

Training on user education and awareness is essential to endpoint security. One of the biggest reasons for security breaches is still human mistake, which frequently results from risky behavior or phishing attempts. Employees can learn about safe computer practices, the most recent risks, and how to spot and report suspicious activity through regular training programs. Promoting a security-aware culture lowers the possibility that social engineering attempts will be effective.

Endpoints are configured as part of endpoint hardening to minimize vulnerabilities and lower the attack surface. This includes setting up security settings, uninstalling unneeded apps, and turning off unused services and ports. By hardening endpoints, attackers find it more challenging to exploit flaws and take over devices.

To identify and address security events, it is imperative to put robust monitoring and tracking procedures into place. Through the acquisition and examination of endpoint logs, entities can detect indications of compromise and implement suitable measures. Endpoint log integration with a Security Information and Event Management (SIEM) system improves the detection of sophisticated threats by enabling centralized visibility and correlation of security events.

Plans for backup and recovery are essential for lessening the damage caused by ransomware and other harmful assaults. Organizations may ensure they can restore their systems and data during a hack by regularly backing up endpoint data. Ensuring that backups are safely stored and inaccessible to hackers is crucial.

Lastly, businesses need to create an incident response strategy that describes what should happen in the case of an endpoint security breach. Procedures for identifying and evaluating events, containing and eliminating risks, restoring compromised systems, and interacting with stakeholders should all be part of this plan. Security teams are guaranteed to be equipped to properly handle real-world circumstances through routine testing and updates of the incident response plan.

To sum up, endpoint protection and response, or EPR, is essential to contemporary cybersecurity tactics. EDR products improve an organization's overall security posture by offering sophisticated capabilities for identifying, addressing, and resolving threats on endpoints. Organizations can effectively safeguard their endpoints against evolving cyber threats by implementing comprehensive endpoint security strategies, including strong access controls, encryption, patch management, endpoint protection platforms, network segmentation, user training, endpoint hardening, monitoring, logging, backup, and incident response planning. Resilient and secure endpoints protect the organization's vital assets and data due to the combination of cutting-edge technology and proactive procedures.

Artificial Intelligence and Machine Learning in Cybersecurity

The increased ability of Artificial Intelligence (AI) and Machine Learning (ML) to detect, evaluate, and respond to more sophisticated cyber threats is transforming cybersecurity. While there are many uses for these technologies that improve security operations, there are drawbacks and ethical questions that need to be considered appropriately.

Many applications of AI and ML exist in cybersecurity, greatly enhancing the efficacy and efficiency of defensive strategies. Threat detection and intelligence is one of the primary uses. Large volumes of data, such as system logs, network traffic, and user behavior, can be analyzed by machine learning algorithms to find patterns that point to potentially harmful activity. ML is capable of identifying abnormalities and zero-day assaults that are missed by rule-based systems, in contrast to conventional signature-based techniques.

Furthermore, automated threat response and mitigation is a strong suit for AI-powered systems. Artificial intelligence (AI) algorithms can detect threats and trigger automatic responses, including quarantining infected data, isolating compromised systems, or blocking harmful communications. By enabling businesses to react to threats instantly, they may lessen the effects of cyber disasters and lighten the strain on human analysts.

Fraud detection and prevention is yet another essential application. Artificial intelligence (AI) algorithms can identify fraudulent behaviors, such as fraudulent transactions or illegal access attempts, by analyzing transactional data, user behavior patterns, and historical records. Financial institutions and e-commerce sites use AI to identify patterns and stop financial losses from cybercrime.

By classifying and evaluating security threats according to the possibility and possible consequences of exploitation, artificial intelligence (AI) also improves vulnerability management. Software and infrastructure vulnerabilities can be predicted by ML models, allowing for proactive mitigation and patching techniques. This proactive strategy improves overall cyber security and narrows the window of vulnerability exposure.

AI also plays a crucial role in improving access control and user authentication systems. AI-powered behavioral biometrics, speech recognition, and facial recognition enhance the precision and security of authentication procedures. Robust identity verification is made possible by these technologies, which lowers the possibility of unwanted access to private systems and data.

Despite their advantages, AI and ML technologies in cybersecurity have several issues that need to be resolved for enterprises to optimize their performance and reduce risks. Adversarial attacks on AI models pose a serious obstacle. By feeding it fraudulent data intended to avoid detection or trick the system into making the wrong judgments, adversaries can influence machine learning algorithms. It takes constant research and development of solid defenses, such as adversarial training and anomaly detection methods, to protect AI models from such attacks.

The difficulty of integrating AI with the current security framework is another obstacle. It frequently takes significant processing power, specialist knowledge, and system integration to implement AI-powered solutions. For enterprises implementing AI in cybersecurity, ensuring compatibility and scalability while preserving operational efficiency presents a significant problem.

Furthermore, worries regarding false positives and false negatives are raised by AI-driven automation. An over-reliance on automated AI systems might lead to inaccurate threat assessments or missed detections, which would be problematic for security teams since they would leave security incidents undetected or generate too many alerts. Automation must be balanced with human monitoring and involvement to guarantee effective threat identification and response.

Concerns about ethics also come up when it comes to AI and ML in cybersecurity. Inadvertent bias perpetuation in training data by AI systems may result in biased threat assessments and user profiles. To minimize ethical hazards and maintain confidence in AI-powered cybersecurity solutions, it is imperative to guarantee equity, openness, and responsibility in AI decision-making processes.

Beyond only addressing technological issues, AI and ML in cybersecurity have wider social ramifications. Invasion of privacy is a significant worry. Unauthorized surveillance and privacy violations are a worry regarding AI-powered surveillance and monitoring systems that can analyze large volumes of personal data. Deploying AI-driven surveillance systems responsibly requires balancing individual privacy rights and security imperatives.

AI also brings up moral concerns about human agency and autonomy. Automated cybersecurity decision-making procedures, like AI-driven incident response or automated threat remediation, may reduce human accountability and control. To control the implementation and application of AI in cybersecurity operations, organizations must set up explicit policies and moral frameworks that guarantee human oversight will always play a crucial role in decision-making.

In addition, the widespread application of AI in cybersecurity raises issues related to national security and geopolitics. The deliberate application of artificial intelligence (AI) in offensive cyber operations and cyberwarfare gives rise to worries about escalation dynamics and unexpected outcomes. International cooperation and legal frameworks are required to solve these issues and encourage the ethical application of AI in cybersecurity.

Furthermore, algorithmic decision-making must be transparent and accountable for AI to be used ethically. Businesses using AI for cybersecurity must make public the workings of their AI systems, the data sources they utilize for training, and the standards by which decisions are made. Transparent AI governance frameworks allow stakeholders to evaluate the dependability and fairness of cybersecurity solutions driven by AI.

In conclusion, by increasing access control mechanisms, automating response activities, enhancing threat detection, and improving vulnerability management, artificial intelligence, and machine learning are revolutionizing cybersecurity. These technologies enable enterprises to efficiently protect against sophisticated cyber threats, offering notable benefits in efficiency, accuracy, and scalability. However, there are drawbacks to using AI in cybersecurity, such as the risk of automation, integration difficulties, adversarial assaults, and ethical issues.

A multidisciplinary strategy including cybersecurity specialists, data scientists, ethicists, legislators, and industry stakeholders is needed to address these issues. Organizations can fully utilize AI and ML while reducing risks by promoting openness and accountability, developing research and development in defensive AI mechanisms, assuring responsible deployment processes, and keeping ethical norms. Ultimately, cybersecurity enabled by AI is a critical development that will help protect digital assets and uphold confidence in the digital economy while opening the door to a more robust and safer cyberspace.

CHAPTER V

Cybersecurity for Cloud Computing

Understanding Cloud Security

Because cloud computing offers scalability, flexibility, and cost-efficiency, it has completely changed how businesses deploy and manage their IT resources. But as companies move more and more vital tasks and sensitive data to the cloud, it's crucial to ensure that solid cloud security measures are in place. To effectively mitigate risks and maintain a safe cloud environment, it is imperative to comprehend the various cloud service models, namely Infrastructure as a Service (IaaS), Platform as a Service (PaaS), and Software as a Service (SaaS), along with their corresponding security implications.

The core of cloud computing is Infrastructure as a Service (IaaS), which offers virtualized computer resources via the Internet. IaaS allows businesses to rent virtualized Infrastructure from cloud service providers (CSPs), which includes servers, storage, and networking components. The operating systems, programs, and data hosted on these virtual computers are entirely under the customers' authority. Although Infrastructure-as-a-Service (IaaS) provides the highest level of flexibility and control, it also heavily burdens the customer with operating systems, applications, and data security within virtual machines. Protecting sensitive data and preventing unwanted access requires the implementation of appropriate access restrictions, network security measures, and encryption methods.

Moving up the stack, Platform as a Service (PaaS) abstracts and offers a platform with databases, middleware, development tools, and other services required to create and run applications. With PaaS, developers can concentrate on creating and maintaining apps rather than worrying about the intricacies of the underlying Infrastructure. Customers protect the apps, data, and user access on the Platform, while PaaS providers handle the underlying Infrastructure and runtime environment. Preventing unwanted access to databases and apps hosted on the PaaS platform entails setting up access controls, doing frequent vulnerability assessments, and implementing safe coding principles.

With the help of Software as a Service (SaaS), businesses can no longer install, maintain, and manage Software locally as it can be delivered over the Internet as a service. SaaS applications include customer relationship management (CRM), enterprise resource planning (ERP) programs, and email and office productivity tools. When using SaaS, the provider manages everything—including data storage and security—and the application infrastructure. Customers are still responsible for setting up user access, maintaining data security regulations, and ensuring legal requirements are met. Monitoring user behavior, securing user credentials, and encrypting data is essential to safeguard sensitive data and control access to SaaS services.

Organizations must consider each cloud service type's distinct security implications to manage risks successfully. Across all cloud service models, data security is the top priority. Putting robust encryption techniques in place for data in transit and at rest is necessary to guarantee data confidentiality, integrity, and availability. Organizations must also implement access controls, authentication procedures, and data loss prevention (DLP) guidelines to stop unwanted access and data breaches.

When processing and storing sensitive data in the cloud, cloud users must ensure that they comply with data protection laws and industry-specific rules. CSPs typically abide by several compliance certifications (such as SOC 2, HIPAA, and GDPR) for their cloud services. Customers must, however, put extra precautions and controls in place to comply with particular legal requirements relevant to their sector and region.

Securing cloud systems requires strict adherence to most minor privilege access guidelines and management of user identities. Insider risks and unwanted access can be avoided by putting multi-factor authentication (MFA), role-based access control (RBAC), and frequent audits of user permissions into place. Robust Identity and Access Management (IAM) procedures guarantee that authorized individuals in the cloud only execute privileged activities and sensitive data.

Strong security measures must be implemented to guard cloud networks against cyberattacks and illegal access. This involves setting up firewalls, intrusion detection and prevention systems (IDPS), and virtual private networks (VPNs) to monitor and manage incoming and outgoing traffic. In the cloud context, network segmentation and the isolation of critical workloads assist in reducing the effect of possible security breaches and attacker lateral movement.

Security events can happen in cloud systems even with precautions taken. It is crucial to have a thorough incident response plan that details discovery, containment, eradication, and recovery processes. Working together, cloud providers and clients can reduce the impact on data integrity and business operations while ensuring prompt incident response.

A key idea in cloud security is the shared responsibility model, which outlines obligations for clients and cloud service providers (CSPs). Distinct cloud service models have different roles assigned to them.

The CSP is in charge of protecting the virtualization layer, underlying Infrastructure servers, storage, networking, and physical data centers. The customers are responsible for securing their operating systems, programs, data, and customizations within the virtual machines.

The CSP with PaaS manages the runtime environment and underlying Infrastructure needed to run apps. Users are in charge of protecting the data, apps, and access controls in the PaaS environment.

The CSP oversees the Infrastructure data storage, and application security of the whole application stack in SaaS. Clients are responsible for setting up user access, carrying out data security procedures, and ensuring legal requirements are met.

To guarantee complete cloud security, the shared responsibility model strongly emphasizes cooperation and open communication between CSPs and clients. Customers install extra security protections and controls unique to their applications and data requirements, while CSPs offer security controls and compliance certifications for their cloud services.

To sum up, comprehending cloud security necessitates having a thorough awareness of the security implications of the three cloud service models: IaaS, PaaS, and SaaS. Data security, compliance, identity and access management, network security, and incident response present different difficulties and factors for each cloud service architecture. Implementing strong security measures, abiding by legal requirements, and using the shared responsibility model to define roles and obligations between CSPs and customers are all part of a proactive approach to cloud security. Organizations may effectively protect their cloud environments and mitigate the risks associated with cloud adoption by using best practices and upholding a collaborative approach. This guarantees the confidentiality, integrity, and availability of their data and applications on the cloud.

Securing Cloud Environments

As more and more businesses move their data and IT infrastructure to the cloud, it is critical to have strong cloud security measures in place to guard against changing cyber threats and vulnerabilities. Using a combination of operational procedures, technical controls, and cutting-edge tools and technologies to protect sensitive data and preserve the integrity of cloud environments means adopting best practices for cloud security.

An organized approach to cloud security can be achieved by putting into practice a recognized framework, such as the Cloud Controls Matrix (CCM) developed by the Cloud Security Alliance (CSA) or the Special Publication 800-53 from the National Institute of Standards and Technology (NIST). These frameworks provide thorough instructions and controls for determining risks, putting security measures in place, and guaranteeing regulatory compliance. Organizations may lay a solid basis for risk management and cloud security governance by adhering to recognized guidelines.

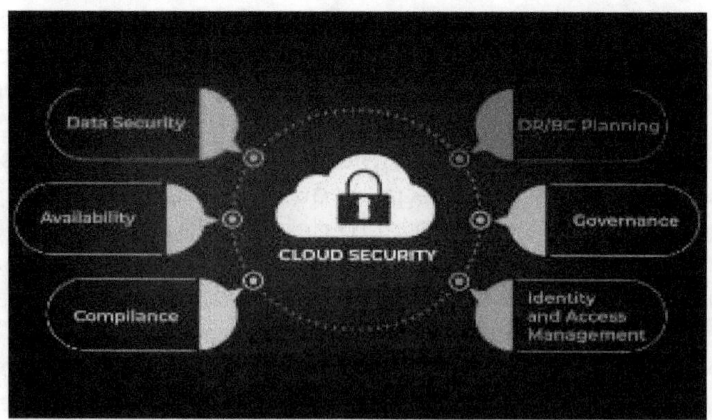

Controlling access to cloud resources and stopping illegal activity requires effective IAM techniques. Enforcing least privilege principles and putting strong authentication measures in place, such as multi-factor authentication (MFA), guarantees that authorized users and apps only access sensitive data and essential tasks. Role-based access control, or RBAC, further restricts permissions based on job positions and responsibilities to lower the risk of insider threats and credential compromise.

It is possible to reduce the possibility of data breaches and unwanted access by encrypting data while it is in transit and at rest. Sensitive data kept in cloud databases, storage services, and virtual machines can be encrypted using native encryption services and critical management solutions provided by cloud providers. By using encryption, you may retain data security and compliance with data protection rules by ensuring that even if data is intercepted or compromised, it remains unreadable without authorized decryption keys.

To guard against unwanted access and cyberattacks, cloud networks must be secured by enforcing strong network security policies. Firewalls, intrusion detection and prevention systems (IDPS), and virtual private networks (VPNs) monitor and regulate incoming and outgoing traffic, instantly spotting and thwarting possible threats. By isolating crucial workloads and apps, network segmentation lessens the effect of security events and stops attackers from moving laterally within the cloud environment.

Real-time cloud environment monitoring and logging gives insight into security incidents, user behavior, and possible threats. Cloud service providers like Amazon CloudWatch, Azure Monitor, and Google Cloud Logging are examples of monitoring tools and services that collect and examine logs for compliance audits, resource usage, and questionable activity. Centralized visibility and correlation of security events are made possible by integrating monitoring with Security Information and Event Management (SIEM) systems. This makes proactive threat identification and incident response easier.

Regular vulnerability assessments and patch management are essential to reduce security risks in cloud systems. Cloud companies often publish security updates and patches to fix known flaws in their infrastructure and services. Organizations should put automated vulnerability scanning tools and workflows into place to quickly find and fix vulnerabilities in virtual machines, containers, and cloud apps. Proactive vulnerability management improves the cloud's overall security posture by minimizing the exposure window to potential exploits.

Creating and testing an incident response plan is crucial to reduce the effects of security incidents and guarantee business continuity in the cloud. Procedures for identifying, containing, and mitigating security breaches, as well as for resuming operations and maintaining data integrity, should all be outlined in the strategy. Cloud providers offer disaster recovery services and backup systems that replicate data across various geographic areas to facilitate quick recovery from data loss or system outages. The efficacy and preparedness of the incident response strategy to handle cyber incidents are confirmed by routine testing.

By implementing security standards across various cloud environments, CASB systems offer visibility and control over cloud apps and services. To safeguard sensitive data and guarantee regulatory compliance, CASBs provide features including data loss prevention (DLP), encryption, access control, and threat detection. Integrating CASB with already-existing IAM and security infrastructure decreases the danger of shadow IT and illegal data exposure, and cloud usage is more visible and under control.

To avoid privilege escalation, container escapes, and unwanted access, enterprises using containerized apps in cloud settings must ensure container security is met. Container security platforms provide runtime protection, vulnerability scanning, and policy enforcement to safeguard containerized workloads and orchestration environments, including Kubernetes. Enhancing the security posture of cloud-native apps and microservices architectures is possible through the implementation of container security technologies and best practices, including image signing, least privilege access, and regular patching.

CWPP solutions offer complete security for serverless operations, virtual machines, containerized applications, and other cloud workloads. Across multi-cloud and hybrid cloud systems, CWPP solutions provide visibility, vulnerability management, runtime protection, and compliance monitoring to secure workloads. Enterprises may safeguard dynamic and scalable cloud infrastructures by combining CWPP with security controls and cloud orchestration tools while guaranteeing constant protection and compliance enforcement.

Specialized security solutions that address particular difficulties like function event injection, unsafe deployments, and resource misconfigurations are needed to secure serverless computing environments, such as AWS Lambda and Azure Functions. Runtime protection, vulnerability scanning, and policy enforcement are provided by serverless security solutions to identify and reduce the risks connected with serverless applications. Secure and reliable serverless deployments in cloud settings are ensured by putting best practices and serverless security tools into effect, such as function isolation, function permissions, and environment-specific security parameters.

Cloud Security Posture Management (CSPM): By automating security and compliance monitoring throughout cloud environments, CSPM systems offer visibility into misconfigurations, policy violations, and configuration problems. CSPM platforms provide ongoing assessment, remedial guidance, and compliance reporting to assist enterprises in adhering to regulatory standards and security best practices. Proactive security posture management is made possible by integrating CSPM with cloud infrastructure-as-code (IaC) frameworks like Terraform and CloudFormation. This guarantees consistent security across cloud installations.

To sum up, protecting cloud environments necessitates a proactive strategy that uses cutting-edge tools and technologies, solid technological controls, and best practices. Organizations can eliminate risks and guarantee the confidentiality, integrity, and availability of their data and applications in the cloud by putting cloud security frameworks into place, embracing IAM principles, encrypting data, protecting networks, putting continuous monitoring and vulnerability management into practice, and getting ready for incident response and disaster recovery. In multi-cloud and hybrid cloud environments, utilizing tools like CSPM platforms, CWPPs, serverless security solutions, CASBs, and container security platforms improves visibility, control, and compliance. Taking a comprehensive approach to cloud security enables businesses to securely negotiate the intricacies of cloud computing and preserve confidence in their digital transformation projects.

Cloud Security Case Studies

Because cloud computing offers scalability, flexibility, and cost-efficiency, it has completely changed how businesses manage their IT infrastructure. However, as enterprises manage intricate threat landscapes and legal constraints, maintaining strong cloud security remains a significant concern. Securing cloud environments may be made more effective by analyzing successful implementations and learning from security breaches. This can help identify problems that need to be solved and lessons that can be learned.

A comprehensive strategy incorporating cutting-edge technologies, proactive risk management techniques, and best practices is necessary for successful cloud security installations. Businesses that have successfully implemented cloud security frequently give top priority to the following crucial areas:

Putting in place robust cloud security frameworks, like the NIST Cybersecurity Framework or the Cloud Security Alliance (CSA) Cloud Controls Matrix (CCM), offers an organized method for identifying risks, putting controls in place, and ensuring that laws and regulations are followed. Organizations facilitate the systematic application of security controls throughout cloud environments by establishing explicit security objectives and governance structures by established frameworks.

Multi-factor authentication (MFA), least privilege access, and centralized identity management are just a few of the IAM concepts that successful cloud security deployments highlight. Organizations reduce the risk of insider threats and illegal access by implementing stringent access controls and monitoring user behavior. By putting in place IAM solutions that work seamlessly with cloud platforms, you can improve visibility and control over user permissions and make sure that only people with the proper authorization may access sensitive information and resources.

Data encryption is necessary both during transmission and at rest to safeguard sensitive data in cloud environments. Organizations use essential management procedures and encryption technology to protect data confidentiality and integrity. To protect client data and uphold confidence, successful implementations also prioritize adherence to data privacy laws, such as the CCPA and GDPR, by putting data masking, anonymization, and privacy-enhancing technology into place.

Effective cloud security tactics depend heavily on the availability of real-time monitoring and threat identification tools. Organizations may immediately discover unusual behaviors, illegal access attempts, and possible security issues by putting monitoring tools, Security Information and Event Management (SIEM) systems, and cloud-native logging solutions into place. Improving insight into cloud infrastructures through continuous monitoring makes proactive threat prevention and quick incident response possible.

Businesses that prioritize these processes are better able to minimize the effects of security breaches and guarantee cloud-based business continuity. Creating thorough incident response plans, doing frequent tabletop drills, and utilizing cloud-based backup and recovery tools are examples of successful deployments. Following security incidents, proactive incident response tactics help firms reduce downtime, restore data integrity, and uphold customer trust.

Even with improvements in cloud security procedures, enterprises still encounter difficulties and gain essential insights from security breaches. Analyzing noteworthy events reveals similar flaws, breaches' underlying causes, and methods for enhancing cloud security resilience:

Inadequate access controls and misconfigurations in cloud services have resulted in several high-profile breaches. Unauthorized parties may unintentionally get access to sensitive data when organizations fail to restrict access permissions or improperly set up security settings. To reduce these risks, it is crucial to apply automated configuration management technologies, carry out frequent security audits, and enforce the least privilege principle.

Robust encryption procedures are crucial, as demonstrated by breaches involving sensitive data that was not encrypted. Businesses that do not encrypt data during transmission or storage in cloud databases risk exposing sensitive data to illegal access and interception. Implementing end-to-end encryption, robust encryption algorithms, and the central management of encryption keys are crucial for efficiently safeguarding data confidentiality, as demonstrated by the lessons learned.

Events involving compromised credentials and insider threats highlight the human element in cloud security flaws. Unauthorized access to data might result from phishing campaigns, weak password practices, or malicious insiders acting on behalf of an organization. To effectively detect suspicious actions and minimize insider threats, it is imperative to deploy behavioral analytics, user behavior monitoring, and continuous security awareness training, as shown by the lessons learned.

Vulnerabilities in supply chains and third-party dependencies are the sources of breaches demonstrating how intertwined cloud ecosystems are. Enterprises that neglect to thoroughly investigate and oversee independent suppliers, APIs, or cloud service providers put themselves at higher risk of cyberattacks and data breaches. To handle supply chain risks proactively, lessons learned highlight the necessity of carrying out extensive vendor assessments, putting contractual security obligations into practice, and creating incident response methods.

The significance of adhering to industry-specific standards and data protection laws is highlighted by breaches that lead to regulatory fines and harm to one's reputation. Sensitive data processing and storage on the cloud presents a challenging set of compliance requirements for businesses in regulated sectors like healthcare and finance. To guarantee conformity to changing regulatory norms, lessons learned highlight the necessity of ongoing compliance monitoring, putting data governance structures into place, and consulting with legal counsel.

In conclusion, enterprises looking to improve their cloud security posture can benefit significantly from analyzing practical implementations and the lessons discovered from security incidents. Thorough security frameworks, robust IAM procedures, data encryption, ongoing monitoring, and proactive incident response planning are all priorities for successful implementations. The significance of resolving common vulnerabilities, including misconfigurations, insufficient encryption, insider threats, third-party risks, and compliance issues, is underscored by lessons learned from breaches. In an increasingly connected and dynamic cloud world, organizations may protect sensitive data, increase cloud security resilience, and efficiently mitigate risks by incorporating best practices, utilizing cutting-edge technology, and learning from prior incidents.

CHAPTER VI

Cybersecurity on the Internet of Things (IoT)

IoT Security Challenges

The Internet of Things (IoT) is a paradigm-shifting technology that links devices to gather, share, and analyze data to automate tasks and improve productivity in various industries. However, because of their particular vulnerabilities and heightened privacy concerns, the proliferation of IoT devices poses serious security difficulties.

IoT devices have unique vulnerabilities that set them apart from conventional computer equipment. These devices include wearable fitness trackers, smart home appliances, industrial sensors, and autonomous vehicles.
Many Internet of Things devices have limited computational resources, such as low amounts of memory, processing power, and storage. These restrictions frequently make it impossible to put strong security measures in place, leaving IoT devices open to abuse by cybercriminals looking to break into them or steal confidential information.

IoT devices frequently use protocols that may need to have built-in security measures or encryption techniques to communicate across wireless networks. Due to flaws in communication protocols, including Bluetooth, Zigbee, and MQTT (Message Queuing Telemetry Transport), Internet of Things devices are vulnerable to illegal access, man-in-the-middle attacks, and eavesdropping by malevolent parties that intercept data transmissions.

Manufacturers routinely release IoT devices with out-of-date firmware or software that might have known vulnerabilities. The likelihood of being exploited by cyber threats, such as malware infections and remote code execution assaults that target unpatched vulnerabilities, is increased in the absence of regular software updates and patch management systems.

Passwords and other default credentials are hardcoded into many Internet of Things devices, and end users hardly ever update or modify them. IoT devices can be compromised by hostile actors using default or weak credentials for credential stuffing attacks, unauthorized access, and device control breaches due to poor authentication procedures and insufficient authorization measures.

IoT devices installed in unmonitored settings, such as industrial control systems and smart city infrastructure, are vulnerable to theft and physical manipulation. Attackers can pose severe risks to infrastructure security and operational continuity by using physical security flaws to obtain unauthorized access to IoT equipment, alter data-gathering procedures, or interfere with vital activities.

Another critical aspect of IoT security difficulties that affects people, businesses, and legal frameworks is privacy concerns:

Massive volumes of data, such as behavioral patterns, sensor readings, and personal information, are constantly being collected and transmitted by IoT devices to third-party platforms or cloud-based servers. IoT devices' vast data-collecting capabilities give rise to worries about widespread surveillance, illegal data access, and possible misuse of private data by hostile organizations or service providers.

Defining ownership rights and getting informed consent for data collection, processing, and sharing are controversial in IoT installations. People frequently need to learn how their data is used by Internet of Things (IoT) devices or how much their personal information can be accessed or used for commercial purposes by third parties without their express authorization. This raises moral and legal questions about data privacy and the protection of consumer rights.

Cybercriminals are always looking to exploit weaknesses in IoT devices that store and communicate personally identifiable information (PII), such as health records, geolocation data, and biometric data. These devices can be used for identity theft, fraud, or unlawful surveillance. Robust encryption, data anonymization strategies, and compliance with data protection laws, such as the California Consumer Privacy Act (CCPA) and the General Data Protection Regulation (GDPR), are necessary to guarantee the confidentiality, integrity, and availability of sensitive personal information (PII).

Organizations implementing IoT devices are subject to strict requirements from regulatory frameworks controlling data privacy and security, such as GDPR, to protect consumer privacy rights, apply data minimization procedures, and maintain openness in data processing activities. Businesses that fail to protect user data and reduce privacy concerns linked with IoT installations risk harsh penalties, harm to their brand, and legal ramifications for not adhering to regulatory demands.

In conclusion, tackling IoT security issues necessitates a multifaceted strategy that includes adhering to privacy-by-design principles, regular firmware upgrades, secure communication protocols, and robust device authentication. To protect consumer rights and IoT ecosystem trust, mitigating privacy problems requires open and honest data practices, informed consent processes, and adherence to changing legislative frameworks. Stakeholders may promote innovation in the digital landscape while ensuring data integrity, confidentiality, and user privacy in an interconnected world by prioritizing cybersecurity and privacy issues throughout the Internet of Things lifespan.

Securing IoT Ecosystems

The Internet of Things (IoT) ecosystems provide distinct security issues because of the wide variety of networked devices and the importance of safeguarding infrastructure and sensitive data. The proliferation of IoT deployments in several areas, including healthcare, manufacturing, smart cities, and consumer electronics, necessitates implementing strong security measures to reduce vulnerabilities and prevent cyber threats.

The cornerstone of IoT security is the implementation of robust access controls and authentication methods. IoT devices should implement least privilege principles and authenticate with solid and unique credentials to restrict access based on user roles and responsibilities. To improve identity verification and reduce the possibility of illegal access and credential theft, multi-factor authentication (MFA) and biometric authentication are used.

Encryption shields Sensitive data against interception and unwanted access when it is in transit and at rest. Robust encryption methods, including Transport Layer Security (TLS) and Advanced Encryption Standard (AES), should be used by Internet of Things (IoT) devices to protect data that is stored in cloud or edge locations and is sent over networks. End-to-end encryption protects against data breaches and manipulation by guaranteeing data confidentiality, integrity, and validity.

IoT devices frequently use protocols like MQTT, CoAP, Zigbee, and Bluetooth to interact via wireless networks. Man-in-the-middle attacks, unauthorized data tampering, and eavesdropping can be avoided by securing communication channels with encryption, mutual authentication, and integrity checks. By implementing secure communication protocols, data exchanges are guaranteed to remain private, and IoT ecosystem integrity is preserved.

Throughout the lifecycle of an IoT device, vulnerabilities must be addressed, and its security must be improved through regular upgrades and patch management. It is recommended that manufacturers promptly release firmware upgrades to address vulnerabilities that have been identified, enhance device functioning, and fortify defenses against new and emerging cyber threats. Patch deployment is streamlined by automated update systems and over-the-air (OTA) upgrades, guaranteeing that devices are safeguarded against constantly changing security threats.

Assigning unique identifiers, keeping track of device configurations, and keeping an eye on operational status from deployment to decommissioning are all part of managing device identities and lifecycles. Centralized device management is made possible by IoT platforms and management systems, which give administrators the ability to verify devices, enforce security regulations, and look for irregularities or illegal changes that can point to compromise.

In high-risk situations, safeguarding IoT devices against physical manipulation and unauthorized access is essential. By putting in place physical security measures like device enclosures, secure boot procedures, and tamper-resistant hardware, one may avoid unwanted tampering and guarantee the integrity of data and device components.

Comprehensive security management features, such as device authentication, policy enforcement, threat detection, and incident response, are provided by specialized IoT security platforms. By integrating with IoT ecosystems, these technologies automate security procedures, enforce adherence to industry norms and laws, and offer real-time visibility into device activity.

IoT-specific endpoint security solutions guard against malware, illegal access, and data espionage. These solutions ensure continuous monitoring and threat mitigation across IoT endpoints by utilizing anomaly detection, machine learning algorithms, and behavior-based analytics to identify and stop suspicious activity.

IoT devices are divided according to their location, purpose, or degree of sensitivity by segmenting IoT networks and installing firewalls. Network segmentation isolates compromised devices from sensitive data and vital infrastructure, reducing the impact of security events and lateral movement. Firewalls improve the overall security posture of IoT deployments by enforcing access control restrictions, monitoring network traffic, and blocking malicious activity.

Blockchain technology improves Internet of Things security by creating decentralized trust, immutability of data records, and transparent transaction validation. Using blockchain-based solutions reduces the dangers of tampering, counterfeit devices, and illegal modifications, and reliance on centralized authorities is lessened for IoT authentication, data integrity verification, and secure firmware updates.

Implementing security measures at the network edge is necessary to secure edge computing settings where IoT data processing occurs closer to devices. In distributed IoT installations, edge security solutions include data encryption, secure data transfer protocols, and local threat detection to guard against unwanted access and guarantee data privacy.

To reduce vulnerabilities and defend against constantly changing cyber threats, securing IoT ecosystems necessitates a proactive strategy that combines industry best practices, strong security measures, and cutting-edge technologies. Organizations can manage firmware updates, prioritize authentication and access control, encrypt data, implement secure communication protocols, prioritize IoT deployment resilience, and protect sensitive data and critical infrastructure by strengthening physical security measures and implementing firmware updates. Embracing comprehensive security strategies and leveraging cutting-edge tools and technologies empowers organizations to embrace the transformative potential of IoT while mitigating risks and ensuring trust in digital ecosystems. Leveraging IoT security platforms, endpoint security solutions, network segmentation, blockchain technologies, and edge computing security enhances visibility, detection capabilities, and incident response readiness across interconnected IoT environments.

Future Trends in IoT Security

IoT ecosystems are excellent targets for sophisticated cyberattacks due to the proliferation of IoT devices, which creates new attack channels and surfaces. Threat actors use poor authentication procedures, unreliable communication protocols, and vulnerabilities in device firmware to obtain unauthorized access, launch ransomware attacks, and compromise private information. New dangers, such as botnets that use Internet of Things (IoT) devices to launch distributed denial-of-service (DDoS) assaults, highlight the necessity of solid security measures to stop disruptions and guard against evil actions that target linked devices.

Maintaining the confidentiality and integrity of data sent and stored by Internet of Things devices is still a significant worry. There are severe threats to people's personal information, corporate data assets, and compliance with data protection laws from privacy breaches, data leaks, and illegal data access. Encrypting sensitive data, using data anonymization methods, and managing it securely reduces privacy threats and increases user confidence in IoT implementations.

Internet of Things ecosystems depend on intricate supply chains that include service providers, component suppliers, and device makers. Implementing supply chain risk management techniques, confirming the integrity of hardware and software components, and building trusting relationships with reliable vendors are all necessary for securing the Internet of Things supply chain. Vulnerabilities that can jeopardize device operation, data integrity, and overall system security are highlighted by supply chain assaults that target Internet of Things devices, such as firmware modification or counterfeit components.

The convergence of IoT with edge computing and cloud services brings new security issues about data processing, storage, and communication. Deploying strong security controls, encryption methods, and access management policies is necessary to secure edge computing environments—where Internet of Things data is processed closer to devices—against unwanted access and data breaches. Ensuring the security and integrity of data exchanged between devices and cloud services requires implementing secure APIs, identity federation, and data encryption when integrating IoT devices with cloud platforms.

To address growing concerns over privacy, data protection, and cybersecurity dangers, governments and regulatory organizations worldwide are focusing more and more on IoT security legislation. Regulations like the US's California Consumer Privacy Act (CCPA) and the EU's General Data Protection Regulation (GDPR) require IoT service providers and manufacturers to adopt secure data handling procedures, privacy-by-design principles, and transparency in data processing activities. Adherence to legislative standards promotes consumer trust, strengthens accountability, and pushes industry adoption of security best practices to reduce the risks associated with Internet of Things deployments.

To create baseline security criteria, interoperability standards, and best practices for IoT deployments, industry consortia, cybersecurity alliances, and international standards organizations develop IoT security standards and guidelines. Consistency in security implementations is encouraged, risk assessments are made more accessible, and organizations are guided in achieving cybersecurity resilience across IoT ecosystems by standards like ISO/IEC 27001 for information security management systems, NIST Cybersecurity Framework, and IoT-specific standards like IoT Security Foundation (IoTSF) guidelines.

Certification programs and compliance frameworks reassure stakeholders, businesses, and consumers by verifying that IoT devices adhere to security guidelines and legal requirements. Certifications that analyze a device's security features, susceptibility, and resilience to known cyber threats include Common Criteria (ISO/IEC 15408) and UL 2900 for IoT cybersecurity. Adherence to certification programs exhibits a dedication to security excellence, bolsters competitiveness in the market, and reduces reputational hazards linked to insecure Internet of Things implementations.

In conclusion, to reduce risks and guarantee the resilience of IoT ecosystems, future developments in IoT security highlight the significance of tackling new threats, improving regulatory compliance, and upholding cybersecurity standards. Organizations must prioritize proactive security measures, such as robust authentication systems, encryption protocols, supply chain security standards, and regulatory compliance, as IoT accelerates across sectors. Adopting cybersecurity standards, certification programs and regulatory frameworks improves cybersecurity posture, encourages innovation of IoT technology, and increases stakeholder trust in the networked digital ecosystem. Incorporating security by design principles and working together across industries and geographical boundaries enable stakeholders to effectively manage changing IoT security concerns, take advantage of the transformative potential of IoT, and protect against new cyber threats.

CHAPTER VII

Regulatory and Legal Aspects of Cybersecurity

Understanding Cybersecurity Regulations

Understanding cybersecurity laws is not just a necessity in today's networked digital world, it's a powerful tool that empowers businesses to protect personal information, reduce cyber threats, and respect the right to privacy for consumers. Laws like the California Consumer Privacy Act (CCPA) and the General Data Protection Regulation (GDPR) provide clear guidelines for companies, giving them control over how they gather, handle, keep, and safeguard personal data. By comprehending these standards, organizations can effectively manage compliance issues and reduce threats to their brand, finances, and legal standing.

The European Union (EU) is enforcing GDPR to protect EU citizens' data and harmonize data privacy rules throughout the continent. It requires companies to get express consent before processing data, to disclose the reasons for data collection, and to put safeguards in place to protect the security and privacy of data. Individuals are entitled under GDPR to view their data, correct errors, and seek deletion (the right to be forgotten). Serious consequences could follow non-compliance, with fines of up to 4% of annual global revenue or €20 million, whichever is larger. This highlights the significance of the rule on the operations of organizations and the stability of their finances.

The CCPA gives Californians more control over the personal information companies may have about them, thereby improving consumer privacy rights. In California, companies that exceed certain revenue thresholds or carry out significant data processing operations must provide information about their data collecting practices, opt-out options for data sales, and grant customers access to the gathered data upon request. The California Civil Code Act (CCPA) forbids discrimination against people who exercise their right to privacy and allows consumers to request that their data be deleted. Businesses must prioritize compliance efforts and strengthen data protection safeguards since non-compliance with the CCPA can result in regulatory fines, civil penalties, and class-action lawsuits.

In addition to GDPR and CCPA, other legislative frameworks that control data privacy in specific industries or regions include the Privacy Act in Australia, the Personal Data Protection Act (PDPA) in Singapore, and the Health Insurance Portability and Accountability Act (HIPAA) in the United States. Healthcare organizations must put administrative, physical, and technical protections to protect patient data by HIPAA, which protects protected health information (PHI). The Personal Data Protection Act (PDPA) regulates the gathering, utilizing, and revealing of personal information in Singapore. It encourages responsible data handling methods and allows people to view and update their data. The Privacy Act ensures accountability and openness in data processing activities by regulating how Australian government entities handle personal information.

Businesses must invest in cybersecurity technologies, undertake regular risk assessments, and implement robust data protection mechanisms to comply with cybersecurity rules. Examples of operational modifications include reorganizing data management procedures, improving IT infrastructure security, and allocating resources to guarantee regulatory compliance. Regarding compliance initiatives, the costs of technology purchases, cybersecurity employee training, and continuous program maintenance are high. Despite practical difficulties, putting compliance first improves an organization's defenses against cyberattacks, fortifies data security procedures, and increases consumer confidence in managing personal data.

In highly competitive marketplaces, demonstrating a commitment to cybersecurity regulations is not just a legal requirement, it's a crucial step in bolstering consumer trust and strengthening brand reputation. Adhering to GDPR and CCPA standards promotes accountability and integrity in customer interactions, including transparency in data procedures, data reduction, and safe data handling. Companies that prioritize data privacy and compliance not only gain the trust of stakeholders, but also reduce the potential damage that data breaches can do to their brand and establish themselves as reliable guardians of personal data. In a time when consumer purchase decisions are influenced by privacy concerns, maintaining a solid reputation for data protection is not just a business strategy, it's a necessity for customer loyalty, sustainable business growth, and increased market competitiveness.

Businesses risk litigation, fines, and legal ramifications when they violate cybersecurity regulations. Regulatory agencies emphasize the financial ramifications of insufficient cybersecurity safeguards by enforcing fines, punishments, and remedial action mandates for violators of data protection regulations. Non-compliance-related data breaches may result in class-action lawsuits, consumer complaints, and a decline in market trust, affecting revenue streams and shareholder confidence. Proactively attending to compliance standards can reduce legal risks, guarantee regulatory compliance, and protect oneself from financial penalties and reputational harm resulting from data privacy violations.

Complying with international cybersecurity laws not only ensures regulatory adherence, but also opens doors for business development and market expansion. While CCPA compliance facilitates interactions with Californian customers, GDPR compliance enables effective functioning within the European market. Global data privacy rules may present regulatory uncertainty, but implementing uniform data protection policies across jurisdictions can enhance cross-border data flows and strengthen relationships with international stakeholders. In a globally networked economy, strategic alignment with cybersecurity standards supports ethical data handling methods, regulatory compliance readiness, and sustainable business growth.

In summary, enterprises must comprehend cybersecurity laws like the CCPA, GDPR, and industry-specific frameworks to successfully manage compliance issues, safeguard customer data, and reduce cyber risks. Organizations must create strong security measures, take a proactive approach to data protection, and maintain openness in their data handling procedures to comply with compliance requirements. Prioritizing cybersecurity rules improves organizational resilience, fosters consumer trust, and reduces legal and reputational risks associated with data privacy violations—all while mitigating the operational difficulties and costs associated with regulatory compliance. Businesses may manage regulatory environments, accomplish compliance goals, and maintain competitive advantage in a changing digital economy by welcoming regulatory constraints as chances to strengthen cybersecurity posture and promote ethical data governance.

Legal Considerations in Cybersecurity

Legal considerations in cybersecurity are critical in determining how businesses safeguard confidential data, respond to cyber threats, and work within regulatory frameworks that protect data privacy and reduce the risks associated with cybercrime in today's interconnected digital landscape. For firms to proactively manage legal risks, uphold regulatory requirements, and maintain customer trust, they must thoroughly understand cybercrime legislation, the enforcement landscape, the legal ramifications of data breaches, and the impact of compliance on businesses.

Cybercrime laws comprise a broad spectrum of legislative actions that combat illegal acts via digital channels. These laws make it illegal to commit crimes, including identity theft, phishing scams, malware distribution, hacking, and cyber extortion. Cybercrime legislation is passed by governments worldwide to prosecute people or organizations that participate in hostile cyber activities that jeopardize data security, interfere with essential infrastructure, or scam customers. Cybercrime laws, which reflect the global commitment to thwarting cyber threats and safeguarding digital assets, give law enforcement agencies the authority to look into cyber occurrences, gather digital evidence, and prosecute offenders.

The effective enforcement of cybercrime legislation and the battle against cross-border cyber threats hinge on international collaboration. Through international treaties, mutual legal assistance agreements, and cybercrime task forces, law enforcement agencies unite to investigate transnational cyber incidents, extradite cybercriminals, and share intelligence on emerging threats. Global initiatives that promote information sharing, capacity building, and coordinated efforts to combat cybercrime on a global scale, such as the Budapest Convention on Cybercrime and INTERPOL's Cybercrime Programme, play a crucial role. Enhanced international cooperation empowers law enforcement to enforce national and international laws more effectively, simplifies cross-border prosecutions, and deters cybercrime that transcends national boundaries.

If a breach involving sensitive personal information occurs, an organization is required by law to notify relevant parties, including affected individuals and regulatory agencies. These rules require the prompt publication of breach information, such as the type of compromised data, the possible effects on impacted parties, and the corrective measures implemented to minimize damage. Data breach management requires proactive breach response and openness to avoid regulatory fines, penalties, and reputational harm from noncompliance with reporting requirements.

When a corporation has a data breach, it may be subject to regulatory inquiries, class-action lawsuits, and civil lawsuits brought by impacted parties, consumer advocacy organizations, or law enforcement. Legal actions resulting from data breaches may bring claims for carelessness, fiduciary responsibility breaches, failure to preserve private information, or infractions of consumer protection legislation. The extent of the financial losses, psychological suffering, and punitive penalties that a court may award depends on the organizational responsibility and the consequences of the data breach. Suppose intentional misbehavior, fraud, or violations of criminal statutes are involved in data breaches. In that case, criminal culpability may result in criminal investigations, prosecutions, and possible incarceration for those responsible. in

Businesses are pressured to put strong security measures in place, protect sensitive data, and adhere to legal requirements to comply with cybersecurity legislation and data protection rules. Conducting risk assessments, putting data protection policies and procedures into place, educating staff members about cybersecurity best practices, and incorporating privacy-by-design ideas into daily operations are all part of compliance activities. Maintaining vigilance over regulatory developments, adjusting cybersecurity procedures to new threats, and proving to stakeholders and regulatory bodies that data handling procedures are accountable are all necessary to achieve compliance.

Noncompliance with cybersecurity standards can lead to severe financial penalties, legal repercussions, and reputational damage. Violations of data privacy regulations can result in hefty fines, with the severity and duration of noncompliance dictating the extent of the penalty. Moreover, inadequate security measures can pave the way for data breaches, eroding consumer trust, tarnishing a brand's reputation, and hampering a company's market competitiveness. By prioritizing regulatory compliance and taking proactive cybersecurity measures, businesses can significantly reduce their exposure to legal risks, bolster organizational resilience, and instill stakeholder confidence in their ability to safeguard sensitive data.

Making cybersecurity compliance a top strategic goal helps organizations stay resilient against cyberattacks and maintain business continuity. Active compliance initiatives reduce operational disruptions brought on by data breaches, improve incident response skills, and facilitate quick mitigation of cyber problems. Organizational preparedness to successfully prevent, identify, and respond to cyber threats is enhanced by investing in cybersecurity technologies, educating staff about cybersecurity, and working with cybersecurity specialists. Businesses may protect their digital assets, respect consumer privacy rights, and preserve confidence in an increasingly interconnected digital economy by prioritizing complying with cybersecurity requirements.

Legal factors in cybersecurity include laws against cybercrime, ways to enforce them, the legal ramifications of data breaches, and how compliance affects companies. Cybercrime laws allow law enforcement organizations to stop hostile cyber activity, safeguard digital assets, and bring legal action against those who engage in illegal cyber activity. Data breach notification regulations emphasize the need for accountability and openness in breach response by requiring prompt disclosure of breaches to affected parties and regulatory bodies. To comply with cybersecurity rules, businesses must put strong security measures in place, protect sensitive data, and reduce the legal and reputational costs of noncompliance. Organizations may improve their resilience against cyber-attacks, maintain consumer trust, and negotiate legal complexity in an evolving digital ecosystem controlled by strict data protection rules by adopting regulatory compliance as a strategic imperative.

The Future of Cybersecurity Legislation

As society grows more dependent on digital technologies, the legal landscape around cybersecurity is expected to undergo significant change, offering benefits and difficulties to organizations, individuals, and policymakers. To effectively reduce worldwide cyber risks, predicted trends in cybersecurity law show a proactive approach to addressing new threats, improving regulatory frameworks, and encouraging international cooperation.

Increased data privacy protections are anticipated to be prioritized in future cybersecurity legislation, driven by increased worries about identity theft, breaches, and unlawful data use. To strengthen consumer rights to data access and deletion, broaden the scope of data categories covered by existing frameworks like the General Data Protection Regulation (GDPR) and the California Consumer Privacy Act (CCPA), and impose more stringent requirements on businesses regarding their data handling practices, legislative efforts may build upon these frameworks. Anticipated reforms seek to provide people more control over their personal information in an increasingly data-driven economy, improve openness in data processing operations, and harmonize data privacy regulations with technology advancements.

The emergence of new technologies such as blockchain, the Internet of Things (IoT), and artificial intelligence (AI) has made regulatory frameworks necessary to handle cybersecurity concerns and ethical issues. To guarantee data integrity, confidentiality, and resistance against cyber threats, future laws may mandate IoT device security requirements, develop standards for the safe deployment and usage of AI algorithms, and set guidelines for applying blockchain technology. Regulations seek to strike a compromise between innovation and cybersecurity requirements, promoting responsible technology advancement and protecting vital infrastructure from new cyber threats brought on by quickly changing digital ecosystems.

Supply chain security is considered a top priority in cybersecurity legislation to reduce the risks related to third-party suppliers, distributors, and service providers. Lawsuits may require vendor due diligence procedures, supply chain risk evaluations, and contractual requirements for adhering to cybersecurity standards. Supply chain relationships should be more transparent and accountable to strengthen organizational resilience against supply chain attacks, data breaches resulting from vendor vulnerabilities, and hostile actions targeting interconnected corporate networks. Legislative initiatives aim to reduce systemic risks brought on by global supply chain interdependence, enhance cybersecurity resilience across industries, and advance supply chain integrity.

Promoting global cybersecurity resilience, enabling cross-border data flows, and harmonizing cybersecurity standards depend heavily on international cooperation. Governments, international organizations, and industry players are working to provide mutually recognized cybersecurity certifications across jurisdictions, unify data protection regulations, and create interoperable cybersecurity frameworks. Globally integrated digital economies benefit from standardized standards because they facilitate frictionless data transfers across borders, simplify compliance for multinational firms, and promote a coordinated strategy for countering cyber threats.

Laws that effectively address cybersecurity promote cooperation and the sharing of threat intelligence across national borders between law enforcement, cybersecurity experts, and businesses. Frameworks for international collaboration allow for the prompt sharing of threat intelligence, coordination of incident response, and collaborative cybersecurity drills aimed at identifying, containing, and attributing cyberattacks that stem from international threat actors. To combat complex cyber threats that target vital infrastructure, governmental institutions, and private sector companies globally, shared cybersecurity information improves situational awareness, fortifies cyber defenses, and encourages coordinated defensive strategies.

Diplomatic initiatives and multilateral agreements aim to define standards and guidelines for responsible state conduct in cyberspace, including cyberwarfare, cyberespionage, and state-sponsored cyber activity. To prevent the escalation of cyber conflicts and maintain global cyber stability, international initiatives such as the United Nations Group of Governmental Experts (UN GGE) on Developments in the Field of Information and Telecommunications in the Context of International Security aim to promote adherence to international law, norms of state behavior, and confidence-building measures. A rules-based approach to cyber governance is encouraged, geopolitical conflicts in cyberspace are lessened, and global cybersecurity cooperation is improved when cybersecurity norms are agreed upon.

In summary, anticipated advancements and trends in cybersecurity law are expected to strengthen supply chain security, regulate new technologies, and improve data privacy protections to counteract rising cyber threats. Harmonizing cybersecurity standards, encouraging cross-border threat intelligence sharing, and creating guidelines for responsible state behavior in cyberspace are all made possible by international cooperation. In an increasingly linked world characterized by digital transformation and cybersecurity imperatives, legislative reforms and cooperative initiatives aim to protect digital economies, enhance global cybersecurity resilience, and respect privacy, security, and accountability principles. In the coming years, stakeholders may traverse new cyber problems, encourage innovation, and guarantee sustainable cybersecurity governance by adopting proactive cybersecurity legislation and promoting international cooperation.

CHAPTER VIII

Building a Cyber-Aware Culture

Importance of Cybersecurity Awareness

Enterprises need to cultivate a cyber-aware culture to successfully minimize cyber threats, safeguard sensitive data, and promote a proactive approach to cybersecurity in the modern digital age. A culture that is cyberaware places a strong emphasis on the importance of cybersecurity knowledge among leaders, stakeholders, and workers, acknowledging their critical role in protecting digital assets and reducing susceptibilities to cyberattacks.

Through cybersecurity awareness efforts, employees and stakeholders are educated on typical cyber threats, the ever-changing threat landscape, and best practices for mitigating security vulnerabilities. Phishing schemes, social engineering techniques, password hygiene, safe data management procedures, and incident response procedures are just a few subjects covered in awareness training courses. Organizations may improve their overall cybersecurity posture and lower the probability of successful cyberattacks by providing people with the information and abilities to recognize possible threats, make educated security decisions, and report suspicious activity.

Cybersecurity awareness encourages employee alertness since it fosters a proactive attitude toward cybersecurity. Acknowledging each person's contribution to safeguarding company data assets motivates staff members to be on the lookout for phishing emails, dubious links, and unwanted access attempts. Fostering a collective responsibility for cybersecurity across all organizational levels and strengthening organizational resilience against cyber threats are achieved by encouraging employees to report security incidents promptly, seek advice from cybersecurity experts, and follow established security policies.

Human factors significantly impact cybersecurity posture since social engineering and behavioral manipulation are common ways cyberattackers take advantage of human weaknesses. Workers may unintentionally reveal private information, click on harmful links, or fall for con artists, jeopardizing company data security. Organizations can reduce the risks associated with human error by implementing targeted cybersecurity training, increasing awareness of emerging threats, and reinforcing a culture of security-conscious behavior by understanding human vulnerabilities.

Organizational cybersecurity is inherently vulnerable to insider threats because workers granted permission to access sensitive data may purposely or inadvertently exploit it for nefarious or personal gain. Behavioral analytics, access restrictions, staff monitoring, and awareness programs that stress ethical behavior, confidentiality duties, and the repercussions of insider wrongdoing are all essential tools for combating insider risks and creating a cyber-aware culture. Building relationships based on trust, encouraging openness in data handling procedures, and creating a positive work atmosphere all deter insider threats and promote adherence to cybersecurity policies and procedures.

By integrating cybersecurity principles into routine business operations, decision-making procedures, and employee behavior, a cyber-aware culture enhances the firm's security posture. To lessen the effects of cyberattacks, proactive risk management, prompt threat detection, and efficient incident response techniques are encouraged by fostering a culture of security awareness.

Businesses that emphasize cybersecurity knowledge and provide staff members the tools they need to advocate for security initiatives strengthen their defenses against changing cyber threats, reduce security lapses, and shield confidential data from exposure or unauthorized access.

Developing a cyber-aware culture makes complying with legal regulations controlling cybersecurity practices, industry standards, and data protection laws easier. Compliance with legal and regulatory requirements is ensured by employees adhering to security rules, data privacy legislation, and incident reporting systems inside the firm. Organizations can exhibit their dedication to safeguarding consumer data, preserving consumer confidence, and reducing legal ramifications from non-compliance or data privacy violations by incorporating cybersecurity awareness into their corporate governance frameworks, risk management plans, and compliance initiatives.

Employees trained to anticipate, address, and recover from cyber disasters are better equipped to strengthen organizational resilience. Giving staff members access to resources, incident response training, and cybersecurity expertise enhances incident management skills and lessens the effect of cyberattacks on corporate operations. Organizations can adapt to changing threat landscapes, minimize operational disruptions, and maintain business continuity in a dynamic digital environment by proactively addressing cybersecurity risks, promoting cross-functional collaboration, and encouraging continuous improvement in security practices.

In conclusion, fostering cybersecurity awareness, reducing human vulnerabilities, and strengthening organizational resilience against cyber threats depend on creating a cyber-aware culture within businesses. Initiatives that raise awareness of cybersecurity threats engage stakeholders, provide staff with the knowledge and skills to make wise security decisions, and foster a proactive attitude toward cybersecurity. Organizations can reduce the risks of insider threats, human error, and malicious behaviors by addressing human elements in cybersecurity. This also helps to create a culture of ethical conduct and security consciousness. Adopting a cyberaware culture improves the organization's security posture, makes regulatory compliance more accessible, and fosters business resilience in an increasingly digitally dependent and networked business environment. By incorporating cybersecurity knowledge into corporate culture, firms better protect digital assets, secure sensitive data, and maintain trust in a cybersecurity environment that is constantly changing due to new cyber threats and ongoing technical breakthroughs.

Training and Education

Any organization's plan to promote growth, guarantee competitiveness, and uphold industry standards must include training and education. Creating effective training programs effective training programs requires a thorough grasp of the company's objectives, the workforce's needs, and the ever changing environment in which the business operates. Campaigns for ongoing education and awareness are essential to keeping the workforce knowledgeable, competent, and prepared to respond to new possibilities and difficulties. This section explores the fundamentals of developing training efforts that have an impact and emphasizes the value of continuous education.

Undertaking a comprehensive needs assessment is the first step towards creating a training program that works. This entails determining the precise knowledge and talent shortages inside the company. Several ways to conduct a needs assessment include surveys, interviews, performance reviews, and requirements analysis. Recognizing these gaps makes it easier to modify the training material to match the specific requirements of the staff, increasing the program's overall effectiveness.

Establishing precise and quantifiable training objectives comes next after needs have been determined. These goals should serve as a guide for trainers and trainees and align with the organization's strategic objectives. For example, the training objectives focus on improving problem-solving, communication, and product knowledge to improve customer service. Well-defined goals guarantee that the instruction stays on target and that results can be efficiently assessed.

Choosing the right training resources and techniques is part of designing the training program. Different training techniques can be used, depending on the abilities that need to be learned. These techniques include workshops, e-learning, classroom instruction, simulation exercises, and on-the-job training. Every approach has benefits. For instance, employees can learn in a real-world setting through on-the-job training, but e-learning offers flexibility and is available at any time.

The training materials should be interesting, current, and relevant. Multimedia components like films, interactive courses, and real-world case studies can improve the educational process. Incorporating subject matter specialists into creating training materials guarantees accurate and thorough content.

A training program that works well includes tools for assessment and feedback—frequent evaluations aid in assessing learner progress and pinpointing areas needing more development. Trainee feedback offers insightful information about the efficacy of the instructional strategies and resources, enabling ongoing program improvement.

Careful preparation and coordination are necessary for the training program's successful implementation. It is crucial to arrange the training sessions at a time when the routine workflow is least disrupted. Trainers should be well-prepared and have the requisite abilities to conduct the training properly. Train-the-trainer sessions can help trainers become more adept at inspiring and involving trainees.

The effectiveness of the training program depends on establishing a helpful learning environment. This entails offering the required tools, including instruction manuals, technological access, and a suitable physical or digital environment for learning. Promoting an ongoing education culture within the company can help the training program work even better.

Employee education and awareness initiatives must be ongoing in today's quickly evolving company environment to keep staff members informed about the newest trends and best practices. These programs support the workforce's continued high degree of competency and adaptability.

Numerous formats are available for continuing education, including seminars, professional development courses, advanced training programs, and certifications. Promoting ongoing education among staff members aids in developing an educated and competent workforce that can lead to innovation and accomplish company objectives.

Campaigns for employee awareness are equally vital in educating staff members about important topics, including cybersecurity, safety, and compliance with company policies. Regular workshops, webinars, newsletters, and instructive sessions can be used to carry out these efforts. The goal is to ensure that staff members are informed about the most recent guidelines, rules, and any dangers to the company.

Technology is essential to improving the efficacy of initiatives for continuous education and training. Training content can be delivered, tracked, and managed using a learning management system or LMS platform. Customized learning pathways, tests, and certifications may be created with an LMS, making it more straightforward to track learner progress.

Platforms for online learning provide an adaptable and affordable option for ongoing education. Workers may manage their work and personal obligations by having access to various courses and learning resources at their speed. Furthermore, the usage of augmented reality (AR) and virtual reality (VR) technology to produce immersive learning environments is growing, especially in industries that demand practical training.

An essential part of any training program is evaluation. It entails assessing the degree to which the training's goals have been met and how the program has affected worker productivity and organizational objectives. Performance metrics, feedback surveys, and pre-and post-training assessments are a few examples of evaluation techniques that can be applied.

The Kirkpatrick Model is a popular paradigm for assessing the efficacy of training initiatives. Reaction, Learning, Behavior, and Results are its four levels. While the Learning level gauges the knowledge and abilities gained, the Reaction level evaluates the trainees' initial response to the instruction. The Results level gauges how the training affects organizational performance, whereas the Behavior level assesses how much the trainees use the newly acquired abilities in their work.

To keep training programs and initiatives for continuous education effective, a continuous improvement approach is necessary. This entails regularly evaluating and revising the training materials, techniques, and content in response to user input and evolving requirements.

Finding fresh ways to improve the training program can be easier by adapting to changing technologies and industry trends.

Additionally, encouraging a feedback culture within the company can yield insightful information for ongoing development. Getting staff members to contribute their ideas and experiences can help find areas where the training program needs improvement and innovation.

Any organization that wants to develop and succeed must create training programs that work and support ongoing education and awareness initiatives. A systematic approach to training that includes requirements analysis, specific goals, exciting material, and frequent assessment guarantees that staff members get the abilities and know-how needed to succeed in their positions. Employees are informed and flexible to new problems by ongoing education and awareness programs, which promote a culture of learning and creativity. Organizations may build a dynamic and productive training ecosystem that improves performance and helps them reach strategic objectives by utilizing technology and implementing a continuous improvement approach.

Leadership and Cybersecurity

Today's digitally-driven world has made cybersecurity a top priority for businesses in every industry. Leadership is critical in supporting and guaranteeing robust cybersecurity procedures as cyber threats become more sophisticated and frequent. Leaders must foster a culture of security in their organizations in addition to determining the strategic path. Understanding the cybersecurity environment, putting strategies into practice, and including every employee in the organization's cybersecurity mission are necessary.

A comprehensive grasp of the threat picture is the first step toward effective leadership in cybersecurity. Leaders must be aware of the different cyber threats, ranging from phishing and malware to more advanced assaults like ransomware and advanced persistent threats (APTs). Leaders can use this information to make well-informed decisions regarding the resources and safeguards required to preserve their company's assets. Leaders who keep up with the newest cybersecurity advancements can better predict potential dangers and take proactive steps to minimize them.

Creating and implementing a thorough cybersecurity plan is one of cybersecurity's most critical leadership responsibilities. This strategy should align with the organization's overall goals and objectives to ensure that cybersecurity measures support and enhance business operations rather than impede them. Data protection, incident response, and disaster recovery policies and procedures are all part of a well-defined cybersecurity plan. It also clarifies the obligations of different parties involved, ensuring everyone knows their responsibility in preserving cybersecurity.

Promoting a security culture within the company is another aspect of leadership involvement in cybersecurity. The values of awareness, accountability, and responsibility form the foundation of this culture. The significance of cybersecurity must be conveyed to all staff members by leaders, who should also emphasize that everyone in the company bears responsibility for it. This includes the IT department. Employees can learn to protect themselves and the company from cyber threats by participating in regular training and awareness initiatives.

A culture of security needs to be promoted by leaders setting an example. This entails acting committed to security in their day-to-day activities and abiding by cybersecurity policies and best practices. Workers are more inclined to follow suit when they witness their superiors taking cybersecurity seriously. To further emphasize the value of security inside the company, management should also honor and commend staff members who exhibit excellent cybersecurity practices.

Providing sufficient resources is a crucial tactic for fostering leadership involvement in cybersecurity. Investments in technology, workforce, and training must be substantial for cybersecurity. Leaders must ensure their company has the right technology and tools to identify, stop, and respond to cyber threats. Examples include firewalls, intrusion detection systems, sophisticated security software, and frequent security audits. Furthermore, companies want knowledgeable cybersecurity specialists to manage these technologies and handle issues successfully. To assemble a strong cybersecurity team, leaders must prioritize attracting, developing, and keeping these experts.

Effective cybersecurity leadership also requires collaboration and communication. Leaders should create open communication channels across all organizational levels and departments to promote knowledge exchange and best practices. By working together, this method guarantees that cybersecurity measures are integrated into all parts of the firm and that everyone is pursuing the same objectives. To stay updated about new risks and exchange information and resources, executives should interact with external stakeholders, including government organizations, industry peers, and cybersecurity specialists.

Crucial components of cybersecurity leadership include incident response and crisis management. To know what to do in a cyberattack, leaders must ensure that their business has a clear incident response plan. This strategy should outline steps for locating and neutralizing the threat, contacting relevant parties, and handling any fallout. Leaders should also regularly run simulations and drills to evaluate the performance of their incident response strategy and make any required modifications. Leaders must maintain composure during a crisis to effectively manage their organization through healing and make wise judgments under duress.

Continuous assessment and development are also essential components of cybersecurity leadership. Organizations must modify their security protocols in response to the ongoing evolution of cyber threats. Leaders should evaluate their cybersecurity strategy regularly, pinpointing areas for development and making the necessary adjustments. This continuous procedure guarantees that the organization maintains a solid security posture and is robust against new threats.

Moreover, executives must push for cybersecurity at the board level and ensure the organization's strategy prioritizes it. This entails giving the board of directors and top executives concise, understandable information regarding cybersecurity risks and their possible effects on the company. By emphasizing the commercial benefits of cybersecurity, executives can obtain the backing and assets required to implement efficient security protocols.

In summary, leadership plays a complex and vital role in advancing cybersecurity, which is crucial for safeguarding an enterprise's digital resources. Leaders must be aware of cybersecurity, create and carry out all-encompassing plans, cultivate a security-conscious culture, assign sufficient resources, and participate in ongoing assessment and development. Through exemplary leadership and a strong emphasis on cybersecurity across all organizational levels, leaders may establish a robust security posture that protects against cyberattacks. Good leadership involvement in cybersecurity keeps the company safe and improves its standing and dependability with stakeholders, partners, and consumers.

CHAPTER IX

Incident Response and Crisis Management

Developing an Incident Response Plan

The unavoidability of cyber incidents in today's digital environment calls for an organized and proactive incident response plan (IRP). With the help of this plan, enterprises may efficiently manage and lessen the effects of cyber events, resulting in a quick recovery and little interruption to daily operations. Creating a successful IRP requires several essential elements, the most important of which are well-defined roles and duties. Organizations comprehending these components can strengthen their defenses against cyberattacks and preserve operational continuity.

The planning stage of an incident response plan is essential for setting the stage for a successful response. Organizations undertake risk assessments, identify possible threats and vulnerabilities, and set up policies and processes for incident response at this phase. Establishing a solid framework that directs the entire incident response process requires this foundational work. This phase is crucial to establishing an incident response team (IRT), establishing event classification standards, and ensuring all the necessary hardware and software are available.

The core of any successful incident response plan is the incident response team. Each team member has a distinct job and responsibility, and they all work together to improve the overall efficacy of the incident response process. The team usually consists of representatives from multiple departments, including communications, IT, legal, and human resources, to guarantee a thorough approach to incident management. The incident response team leader, frequently a senior IT or security specialist, manages the team's activities, making tactical choices and monitoring the incident response process.

Clearly defining roles and duties within the incident response team is essential. Every team member must know their responsibilities and how they fit into the more significant response effort. For instance, IT staff members usually locate and neutralize threats, while legal professionals handle compliance and regulatory matters. Human resources specialists handle any employee-related concerns during the crisis, while communication specialists oversee internal and external communications to guarantee accurate and fast information distribution. Organizations can guarantee a well-coordinated and effective response to incidents by clearly defining these responsibilities.

An effective incident response strategy also needs to include detection and analysis. Monitoring systems and networks for potential incidents, such as abnormal network traffic, illegal access attempts, or data breaches, is the focus of this phase. In this process, advanced detection technologies, including endpoint detection and response (EDR) tools, intrusion detection systems (IDS), and security information and event management (SIEM) solutions, are essential. As soon as an incident is discovered, the incident response team must act quickly to assess the threat's nature and extent.

During the analysis phase, incident responders collect and review evidence to comprehend attack pathways, impacted systems, and possible consequences. Forensic analysis is frequently used in this process to determine the cause of the occurrence and evaluate the damage. Making judgments regarding the incident response process's future stages requires quick and accurate analysis. This effort is coordinated by the incident response team leader, who makes sure that all pertinent data is gathered and examined to direct the containment and eradication operations.

During the containment phase, the incident response team takes steps to reduce the incident's impact and spread. This entails putting in place temporary safeguards to stop additional harm, blocking malicious IP addresses, and isolating impacted systems. Containment tactics come in two flavors: short-term and long-term. While long-term containment entails more extensive efforts to guarantee the threat is completely neutralized, short-term containment seeks to stop the threat immediately. Clear communication and teamwork are essential for effective confinement to carry out the required tasks quickly and effectively.

After containment, the eradication phase concentrates on eliminating the incident's primary cause. This includes eradicating malware, patching vulnerabilities, and updating systems impacted by security flaws. To stop re-infection, the incident response team must eliminate the threat. A thorough recording of the eradication process is necessary for learning and future reference. Before the recovery phase, the team leader ensures that all actions are fully recorded and that the organization's systems are secure.

Recovery is the stage in which the company returns to regular business while confirming the integrity of any compromised systems. This includes verifying system functionality, restoring data from backups, and ensuring security precautions are reinforced to avert similar occurrences in the future. Recovery procedures must be well-planned and carried out to reduce downtime and guarantee a smooth return of business activities. Throughout this phase, it is crucial to monitor for any indications of persistent dangers and confirm that the recovery efforts are working.

An efficient incident response strategy must include post-event activity. To determine the lessons learned and potential areas for development, a comprehensive evaluation of the incident and the response procedure is conducted during this phase. A post-incident report should be written, explaining the incident's nature, the steps taken in response, and any flaws or holes found in the IRP. This report is an excellent tool for improving the organization's cybersecurity posture and incident response plan. In charge of overseeing this review and making sure all insights are recorded and used, is the incident response team leader.

Ongoing initiatives to enhance the efficacy of the incident response plan include raising awareness and providing training. The incident response team and other staff members participate in regular training sessions to ensure everyone knows their duties and responsibilities. Tabletop drills and simulation exercises help validate the plan and prepare the team for real-world situations. All staff are updated on cybersecurity through ongoing training and awareness programs, emphasizing the value of being watchful and taking preventative action.

To sum up, creating a successful incident response plan requires several essential elements, the most important of which is clearly defined roles and duties. Organizations may create a robust framework for handling cyber incidents by planning ahead of time, assembling a capable incident response team, and guaranteeing efficient detection, analysis, containment, eradication, recovery, and post-incident operations. The plan's efficiency is further enhanced by ongoing training and awareness campaigns, guaranteeing that all stakeholders are prepared to react to cyber threats quickly and efficiently. By implementing these all-encompassing measures, entities may safeguard their resources, preserve uninterrupted operations, and establish a resilient barrier against the always-changing realm of cyber hazards.

Crisis Management in Cybersecurity

In the digital transformation era, cybersecurity crises have become a prevalent threat to organizations globally. Major cyber incidents, such as data breaches, ransomware attacks, and denial-of-service attacks, can affect an organization's operations, reputation, and bottom line. Effective crisis management in cybersecurity is essential to mitigate these impacts, ensure swift recovery, and maintain stakeholder trust. A key component of successful crisis management is the implementation of robust communication strategies that guide the organization through the turmoil and facilitate transparent and efficient information flow.

Handling major cybersecurity incidents begins with thorough preparation. Organizations must establish a comprehensive crisis management plan that outlines the steps to be taken during a cyber incident. This plan should include detailed procedures for incident detection, assessment, containment, eradication, and recovery. Preparation also involves forming a dedicated crisis management team (CMT) comprising members from various IT, legal, public relations, and senior management departments. This team oversees the crisis response, makes critical decisions, and coordinates efforts across the organization.

When a significant cyber incident occurs, swift and decisive action is paramount. The first step is to identify and assess the nature and scope of the incident. This involves gathering as much information as possible about the attack, including its origin, the systems affected, and the potential impact on the organization. Rapid detection and assessment are crucial for determining the appropriate response measures and minimizing damage. The crisis management team must work closely with IT and cybersecurity professionals to analyze the threat and develop an effective containment strategy.

Containment is a critical phase in crisis management, as it aims to limit the spread and impact of the cyber incident. Depending on the nature of the attack, this may involve isolating affected systems, blocking malicious IP addresses, and implementing temporary security measures. The crisis management team must ensure that containment efforts are communicated clearly and effectively to all relevant stakeholders, including employees, customers, and partners. This communication should be timely, accurate, and transparent, providing stakeholders with the information they need to understand the situation and take necessary precautions.

Effective communication strategies during a cybersecurity crisis are essential for maintaining trust and credibility. The crisis management team must develop a communication plan outlining how information will be disseminated internally and externally. Internally, informing employees about the incident and the steps to address it is essential. Regular updates should be provided through email, intranet, and team meetings. These updates should be clear and concise, providing employees with actionable information and reassurance that the organization handles the crisis effectively.

Externally, communication with customers, partners, regulators, and the public is equally important. The crisis management team should designate a spokesperson from the public relations or communications department to serve as the primary point of contact for external stakeholders. This spokesperson should provide regular updates on the incident, including its impact, the actions to resolve it, and any measures stakeholders need to take. Transparency is critical to maintaining trust, so it is essential to be honest about the damage's extent and the steps to mitigate it.

One of the most challenging aspects of communication during a cybersecurity crisis is managing the flow of information in real-time. The crisis management team must establish a centralized communication hub where all information related to the incident is collected, analyzed, and disseminated. This hub is the single source of truth, ensuring that all communications are consistent and accurate. It is also essential to monitor social media and other public channels for misinformation and rumors, addressing them promptly to prevent confusion and panic.

Crisis communication should also be tailored to the needs and concerns of different stakeholders. For example, customers will be primarily concerned about their personal information's security and the steps to protect it. Partners may be worried about the impact on their operations and the continuity of their business relationship with the affected organization. Regulators will need detailed information about the incident and the measures being taken to comply with legal and regulatory requirements. By understanding each stakeholder group's specific needs and concerns, the crisis management team can tailor their communication efforts to address these issues effectively.

In addition to managing immediate communication needs, the crisis management team must focus on long-term reputation management. A well-handled crisis can enhance an organization's reputation, demonstrating its commitment to transparency and customer protection. Conversely, poor communication and inadequate crisis handling can negatively affect an organization's brand and trustworthiness. After resolving the immediate crisis, the organization should thoroughly review the incident and its communication strategies. This review should identify what worked well, what could be improved, and any lessons learned to inform future crisis management efforts.

Training and preparedness are crucial for effective crisis management and communication. Organizations should conduct regular crisis simulations and drills to test their incident response and communication plans. These exercises help identify potential weaknesses and areas for improvement, ensuring that the crisis management team is well-prepared to handle real-world incidents. Training should also include media training for designated spokespersons, ensuring they can handle press inquiries and public statements confidently and effectively.

In conclusion, crisis management in cybersecurity requires a comprehensive and proactive approach to handling significant incidents and implementing effective communication strategies. Preparation is vital, with detailed crisis management plans, dedicated teams, and regular training exercises forming the foundation for a successful response. During a crisis, swift detection, assessment, and containment are critical, supported by clear, transparent, and tailored communication with all stakeholders. By managing the flow of information effectively and maintaining trust and credibility, organizations can navigate cybersecurity crises successfully, minimizing damage and ensuring swift recovery. Continuous review and improvement of crisis management and communication strategies enhance organizational resilience, ensuring preparedness for future incidents.

Post-Incident Recovery and Analysis

An organization's cybersecurity strategy must include efficient post-incident recovery and analysis because cyber threats are constant in the digital era. Following a cybersecurity event, recovery and analysis become more essential than quick reaction and containment. During this phase, regular operations must be resumed, risks must be reduced going forward, and lessons must be learned from the incident to avoid a repeat. Enhancing an organization's overall cybersecurity posture and resilience requires implementing recovery procedures and post-incident evaluation processes.

The first stage in post-event recovery is ensuring the safe restoration of all impacted systems and data. This entails a detailed analysis of how the incident affected the organization's data, operations, and IT infrastructure. IT staff put a lot of effort into finding compromised systems, removing them from the network, and replacing or restoring them as needed. Reinstalling operating systems, installing security updates, and retrieving data from backups are a few examples of this. Return to regular operations is the aim as soon as safely and swiftly as feasible, and all vulnerabilities exploited during the incident must be fixed.

It's still crucial to communicate during the recuperation stage. It is imperative to provide stakeholders, such as staff members, clients, associates, and authorities, with updates regarding the progress of the recovery activities and any possible consequences for their engagements with the company. Two benefits of transparent and timely communication are ensuring that the company is efficiently addressing the crisis and preserving trust. Regular updates to staff members about internal communication can assist in sustaining morale and guarantee that everyone is aware of ongoing recovery efforts. It is crucial to clearly and concisely communicate to the outside world what went wrong, how it is being fixed, and what is being done to stop such situations in the future.

Improving security protocols to avert future occurrences is critical to incident recovery. This entails putting in place extra security measures, revising policies and guidelines, and sometimes investing in new technology. Suppose a phishing assault caused the incident, for instance. In that case, the company might improve its email filtering capabilities and provide staff members with more training to spot phishing attempts. It becomes crucial to ensure that all systems are routinely updated and patched if a software vulnerability caused the occurrence. By taking lessons from the current situation, the aim is to create a more robust defense against such attacks in the future.

A comprehensive post incident review becomes the primary priority when regular activities have resumed. Understanding what happened, why, and how it might be averted depends on this review process. The thorough post-event review should include all parties involved in the incident response. This includes management, legal and compliance staff, IT and security teams, and any outside partners or consultants that were engaged.

Compiling all pertinent information concerning the occurrence is the first stage in the post-incident review process. Logs, alarms, and any other data that can provide light on the circumstances and consequences of the occurrence fall under this category. A thorough report of their activities, including what was done, when it was done, and the results of those actions, should be assembled by incident response teams. A detailed investigation of the occurrence is predicated on these data.

An investigation of the root cause is the next stage. This entails figuring out the incident's fundamental causes instead of just its symptoms. For instance, if a password compromise led to a data breach, a weak password policy, or insufficient user education on password security may have been the primary contributing factor. Organizations can prevent such disasters in the future by implementing more effective long-term remedies by addressing the underlying reasons.

Assessing the incident response's efficacy is crucial to the post-event review. This entails evaluating the effectiveness of the communication, the timeliness and scope of the recovery activities, and the incident response plan's execution. All of the parties' input is very important to this assessment. Organizations can identify areas for improvement and adjust their incident response plans by learning about what worked and what didn't.

Evaluating the incident's influence on the organization is crucial to the post-incident review. This covers immediate effects like monetary losses and system outages and long-term effects like damaging one's reputation and diminished customer confidence. Comprehending the complete extent of the impact facilitates the development of plans by organizations to mitigate similar consequences in future crises. It also offers valuable information for insurance and risk management.

An actionable set of recommendations should be developed by companies based on the results of the post-incident evaluation. The suggestions above should tackle the recognized vulnerabilities and delineate measures to enhance the overall cybersecurity posture. This could involve organizational and technical steps, like improving staff awareness and training initiatives and implementing cutting-edge threat detection technologies. Prioritizing these suggestions according to their potential influence and viability is crucial.

Continuous improvement depends on putting the post-incident review's recommendations into practice. To make sure that the suggested modifications are successfully incorporated into the organization's operations, this process needs to be closely watched. Frequent follow-up evaluations can assist in monitoring development and implementing any necessary corrections. The intention is to establish a continuous improvement cycle in which every event yields insightful lessons that fortify the organization's defenses against potential dangers.

Organizations could also consider hiring outside auditors and assessors in addition to internally conducted reviews. Outside specialists can offer an unbiased viewpoint and identify problems internal teams might miss. These audits can provide more suggestions for development while also confirming the efficacy of the company's incident response and recovery operations.

To summarize, post-event recovery and analysis are critical elements of a successful cybersecurity plan. Restoring compromised systems, strengthening security protocols, and keeping open lines of contact with relevant parties are the phases of the recovery process. Organizations can better comprehend the underlying causes of incidents, assess the success of their response, and create meaningful improvement recommendations by carrying out comprehensive post-incident evaluations. Organizations may strengthen their resilience against future cyber threats and secure long-term success in an increasingly digital world by continuously improving their security posture and learning from each occurrence.

CHAPTER X

The Future of Cybersecurity

Predicting Future Threats and Trends

Anticipating future cybersecurity threats and trends is essential to sustaining solid defenses in the quickly changing digital realm. While emerging technologies present never-before-seen chances for efficiency and creativity, they also create fresh points of vulnerability and entry for online criminals. One must understand these technologies and their ramifications to build proactive security measures and prepare for future threats.

Artificial intelligence (AI) is one of the most revolutionary new technologies. Because AI and ML enable predictive analytics, automated responses, and better threat detection, they have the potential to transform cybersecurity completely. AI-driven systems can analyze massive data sets to find trends and abnormalities that might point to a cyber threat. AI, for instance, can identify anomalous network traffic and warn of possible viruses or intrusions that conventional security systems could miss. Cybercriminals can, however, use the same qualities that make AI a potent tool for cybersecurity. Adversaries can use AI to create complex malware, automate assaults, and surpass traditional security measures. AI-driven attacks are a new severe threat that businesses must be ready for. One example is the deep fake technology used in social engineering.

Another significant development changing the cybersecurity landscape is the emergence of the Internet of Things (IoT). IoT devices are becoming more commonplace; they can be anything from industrial sensors to smart home appliances. Because these devices frequently have few security protections, fraudsters find them appealing targets. Because IoT ecosystems are interconnected, a flaw in one device might compromise a whole network. The potential attack surface increases with IoT growth, necessitating robust security protocols and ongoing monitoring to prevent breaches. Large-scale attacks on vital infrastructure via infiltrated IoT devices could be among future challenges, highlighting the necessity of secure device management and network segmentation.

Cryptocurrencies first popularized blockchain technology, which also impacts upcoming cybersecurity trends. The decentralized and unchangeable ledger blockchain system presents interesting uses for identity management and safe data transactions. Blockchain, for instance, can improve supply chain security by offering tamper-proof, transparent records of product origins and transactions. Blockchain technology is not impervious to attacks, though. Cybercriminals may be able to take advantage of flaws in smart contracts, which are blockchain-based automated agreements that enforce rules. Furthermore, money laundering and financing cybercrime are illegal acts that can benefit from blockchain's anonymous qualities. As the technology advances, comprehending these vulnerabilities and creating safe blockchain protocols will be essential.

Another revolutionary technical development that has a significant impact on cybersecurity is quantum computing. Complex mathematical problems could be solved by quantum computers exponentially faster than by traditional computers. Although this capability presents substantial risks, it also holds great promise for fields like cryptography. Because commonly used cryptography systems may be broken by quantum algorithms, quantum computing may make present encryption techniques obsolete. To protect data from future quantum-enabled attacks, it is necessary to design encryption algorithms resistant to this possible vulnerability. In the upcoming years, cybersecurity professionals will focus heavily on shifting to post-quantum cryptography.

5G network integration is expected to transform communication by offering faster speeds, reduced latency, and the ability to connect many devices simultaneously. But the introduction of 5G also brings with it new security issues. Cyber threats have more opportunities due to the expanded attack surface and improved bandwidth and device connectivity. Moreover, adversaries can take advantage of additional vulnerabilities brought about by the complexity of 5G networks due to their reliance on network function virtualization (NFV) and software-defined networking (SDN). Comprehensive security measures, such as solid encryption, ongoing monitoring, and stakeholder participation, will be necessary to secure 5G infrastructure.

Another developing trend with consequences for cybersecurity is the emergence of edge computing, which analyzes data closer to its source rather than in centralized data centers. Edge computing is crucial for applications such as driverless vehicles and smart cities because it lowers latency and enhances real-time data processing. However, edge computing's decentralized architecture makes data security and privacy more difficult. Robust security frameworks that adjust to changing conditions are necessary to protect data across multiple edge devices and locations. As this technology spreads, protecting the confidentiality and integrity of data at the edge will become increasingly important.

Biometric authentication—including voice, facial, and fingerprint recognition—is becoming increasingly popular as a safer substitute for conventional passwords. Because biometrics rely on distinct physical traits that are hard to copy, they provide increased security. However, the usage of biometric data brings with it risks of data breaches and privacy issues. Unlike passwords, biometric data cannot be altered once compromised, which could result in long-term security problems. As biometric authentication spreads, it is crucial to guarantee the safe transmission and storage of biometric data in addition to strong encryption and privacy safeguards.

Cloud computing, which provides scalable and adaptable options for processing and storing data, is still a significant trend in the IT industry. But moving to cloud environments also means dealing with fresh security issues. Data security is a shared duty between cloud providers and consumers, which may lead to security coverage gaps. Insider attacks, misconfigurations, and data breaches are significant issues in cloud settings. Creating thorough cloud security plans that include strong access controls, encryption, and ongoing monitoring will be essential to reducing risks as businesses depend more and more on cloud services.

Another concern for future cybersecurity is social media platforms and their impact on information transmission. Social media is used by social engineering attacks, like phishing and disinformation campaigns, to target people and businesses. Cybercriminals create tailored assaults utilizing the abundance of personal information on social media. The proliferation of false information and fake news presents more dangers since it can sway public opinion and cause extensive disruption. Improving digital literacy, imposing more stringent security measures on social media sites, and providing tools for identifying and dispelling false information is imperative to solve these issues.

In conclusion, the quick development and uptake of new technologies will continue influencing the cybersecurity threat landscape. Although there are many advantages to emerging technologies, companies also need to be aware of the latest dangers and vulnerabilities they present. Security issues are specific to artificial intelligence, the Internet of Things (IoT), blockchain, quantum computing, 5G, edge computing, biometric authentication, cloud computing, and social media. Organizations must take a proactive approach to cybersecurity to be ready for the future. This includes closely monitoring the threat landscape, investing in cutting-edge security solutions, and promoting a security-aware culture. Organizations may fortify themselves against the dynamic risks of the digital era by comprehending the consequences of developing technologies and putting strong security measures in place.

Innovations in Cyber Defense

The development of cyber defense technology must always continue, given the dynamic nature of cyber threats. Thanks to state-of-the-art research and development, innovative defensive solutions are being developed in this field to shield organizations against ever more sophisticated attacks. These developments cover a broad spectrum of technology, including blockchain, quantum computing, and artificial intelligence as well as machine learning. Gaining an understanding of these developments is essential to creating robust cybersecurity plans that can successfully fend off threats in the future.

Machine learning (ML) and artificial intelligence (AI) lead cyber protection innovations. Because they enable automated threat identification and response, these technologies have the potential to revolutionize cybersecurity. AI-powered systems can instantly analyze Massive amounts of data and then spot trends and abnormalities that could point to a cyber threat. Machine learning algorithms, for example, can identify anomalous network traffic and indicate possible viruses or intrusions. Furthermore, by evaluating past data and seeing new dangers before they manifest, AI can assist in anticipating and averting cyberattacks. Artificial intelligence (AI) is a potent weapon in the battle against cybercrime because of its capacity to learn and adapt constantly.

Creating sophisticated intrusion detection systems (IDS) is one of the most promising uses of AI in cybersecurity. These systems achieve real-time threat detection and response through machine learning. The signature-based detection method traditional IDS uses is frequently unreliable against novel and unidentified threats. On the other hand, AI-driven intrusion detection systems offer more dynamic and proactive security by identifying behavioral patterns linked to hostile actions. AI can also improve incident response by automating repetitive processes, allowing human analysts to work on more complex problems.

Another innovative technology with great potential for cyber defense is quantum computing. Unlike traditional computers, quantum computers can answer complicated mathematical problems far more quickly. This ability can create new encryption techniques that fend off attacks from both quantum and classical computers. For instance, quantum key distribution (QKD) creates secure communication channels impervious to eavesdropping by utilizing quantum mechanics concepts. To protect data from upcoming quantum-enabled assaults, developing and applying quantum-resistant encryption solutions as quantum computing technology develops will be crucial.

Initially created for cryptocurrency, blockchain technology now finds cutting-edge cybersecurity uses. Blockchain is the perfect answer for safeguarding data transfers and identity management since it is decentralized and irreversible. Blockchain can improve security in several applications, including digital identities, voting systems, and supply chain management, by offering a transparent and unchangeable record of transactions. Self-executing contracts, or smart contracts, are recorded on the blockchain and have the potential to improve security by automating and enforcing terms of contracts without the need for intermediaries. Still, a crucial research topic is how to protect blockchain apps from potential flaws like brilliant contract exploitation.

Creating zero-trust architecture is a noteworthy advancement in cyber security (ZTA). The zero-trust model functions because no entity—internal or external to the network—should be trusted by default. Instead, it necessitates ongoing user identity and access privilege verification. In the event of a breach, this strategy helps to stop lateral movement inside the network, lowering the possibility of extensive damage. Using technologies like sophisticated access restrictions, micro-segmentation, and multi-factor authentication (MFA) is part of implementing ZTA. Modern cybersecurity methods increasingly rely on the zero-trust concept as more and more enterprises utilize cloud services and work remotely.

Edge computing is another cutting-edge technology that significantly impacts cyber protection. Edge computing enhances real-time data analysis and lowers latency by processing data closer to its source. This decentralized strategy improves security by establishing many levels of defense and minimizing the quantity of sensitive data transferred over networks. But protecting edge devices, which frequently have low processing and storage capacity, offers particular difficulties. This field's research aims to provide encryption techniques and lightweight security protocols to safeguard data at the edge without sacrificing efficiency.

The incorporation of biometric authentication techniques is also advancing cyber protection. Compared to standard passwords, biometrics—such as voice, facial, and fingerprint recognition—offer a more secure option. Because biometric verification is based on distinct bodily traits that are hard to copy, there is less chance of unwanted access. However, privacy issues and misuse potential are associated with using biometric data. With the increasing adoption of these technologies, it is imperative to guarantee the safe transmission and storage of biometric data, in addition to strong encryption and privacy safeguards.

Creating sophisticated threat intelligence platforms is a crucial area of innovation. These platforms gather, examine, and disseminate data from various sources, such as open-source information, proprietary databases, and industry partnerships, regarding currently active or developing risks. Threat intelligence solutions can help organizations proactively protect against cyberattacks by using big data analytics and machine learning to deliver actionable insights and predictive analytics. Sharing threat intelligence amongst various industries and institutions improves defense efforts and facilitates more efficient threat identification and mitigation.

The emergence of 5G technology is poised to transform communication by offering faster speeds, reduced latency, and the ability to connect many devices simultaneously. However, the introduction of 5G networks also brings new security issues. Cyber threats have more opportunities due to the expanded attack surface and improved bandwidth and device connectivity. Researchers are creating sophisticated encryption techniques, secure communication protocols, and improved network monitoring tools to safeguard 5G infrastructure. Since 5G networks will serve as the foundation for all future connectivity and communication, it will be imperative to ensure their security.

Programs for cybersecurity awareness and training are also developing thanks to cutting-edge technologies.

Employing virtual reality (VR) and augmented reality (AR), immersive training environments that mimic actual cyberattack scenarios are being developed. Professionals in cybersecurity can gain practical experience from these simulations, which aid in developing and refining their abilities in a safe environment. Furthermore, gamification strategies enhance training's effectiveness and engagement while motivating staff members to acquire and use sound cybersecurity practices.

To sum up, cutting-edge research and development in fields like artificial intelligence (AI), quantum computing, blockchain, zero-trust architecture, edge computing, biometrics, threat intelligence platforms, and 5G propels cyber protection advancements. These developments present fresh and more potent means of thwarting cyberattacks but also bring new difficulties that need to be solved. Organizations may improve their cybersecurity posture and strengthen their defenses against future assaults by keeping up with the latest technology advancements and constantly adjusting to the changing threat landscape. Protecting digital assets and guaranteeing the security of our increasingly interconnected world will need the integration of this cutting-edge technology together with thorough training and awareness campaigns.

The Role of Collaboration and Global Efforts

The need for international cooperation in tackling global security issues has grown in an increasingly interconnected world. Threats have expanded from conventional state-centric wars to include a broad range of problems such as pandemics, cyberattacks, terrorism, and climate change. These complex dangers highlight the vital need for international cooperation and call for a collective defense plan. Thus, maintaining international collaboration is advantageous and necessary for preserving world security and stability.

Realizing that no country can handle all security issues on its own, no matter how powerful, is the foundation of international defense cooperation. Modern dangers are complex and interdependent, necessitating skills, resources, and knowledge sharing. In the area of cybersecurity, this is clear. Because cyber dangers cut across national boundaries, it is crucial that nations work together to share intelligence, create shared defenses, and set global standards for acceptable cyber behavior. Regional cooperation can strengthen collective defense capabilities, as demonstrated by the European Union's attempts to improve cybersecurity by establishing the European Cybersecurity Industrial, Technology, and Research Competence Centre.

International collaboration promotes transparency and trust between states, which is essential for maintaining world peace and security. Arms control agreements and joint military drills are two examples of trust-building initiatives that help allay fears and stave off confrontations. For example, the NATO-Russia Founding Act on Mutual Relations, Cooperation, and Security was created to create a stable, peaceful, and united Europe. Geopolitical conflicts have tested this relationship, but the framework emphasizes how crucial communication and collaboration are to preserving security.

Sharing resources and capabilities is one of the most important parts of international defense cooperation. By pooling their resources, nations can make their military plans more effective and efficient. This is especially important for smaller or less developed countries, as they might need more resources to develop cutting-edge defense technologies independently. Member states gain access to collective defense agreements—in which an assault on one is viewed as an attack on all—through alliances like NATO. In addition to discouraging possible aggressors, the collective defense principle guarantees that member states can depend on the alliance's protection during difficult times.

To promote collaboration and develop collective defense plans, international organizations are essential. For example, the United Nations (UN) offers a forum for discussion and conflict resolution, assisting in reducing tensions before they become significant confrontations. The UN's peacekeeping operations, which combine forces and resources from several nations to pacify conflict areas and safeguard civilians, are a tribute to the effectiveness of collective action. These missions show how international collaboration can successfully handle security issues that individual countries might find difficult to handle independently.

International defense cooperation also benefits significantly from the efforts of regional organizations. The African Union (AU) takes action to avert and end wars on the continent through the Peace and Security Council. Comparably, the Association of Southeast Asian Nations (ASEAN), which fosters cooperation and communication on security-related matters through platforms like the ASEAN Regional Forum, works to advance regional stability. To ensure a complete approach to security that tackles both the local and international elements of threats, these regional measures are in addition to global initiatives.

The battle against terrorism exemplifies how international collaboration is essential to developing a collective defense plan. Terrorist networks are transnational organizations that plan and carry out attacks via international financial and communication networks. Thus, a concerted worldwide reaction is necessary for counterterrorism measures to be effective. The effectiveness of coordinated action is exemplified by initiatives such as the Global Coalition to Defeat ISIS, which unites more than 80 nations and organizations. The alliance has made significant progress in weakening ISIS's capabilities through coordinating efforts to cut off funding and resources to terrorist organizations, exchanging intelligence, and conducting combined military operations.

Global security also depends on international cooperation in the domain of climate change. Global stability is seriously threatened by the effects of climate change, including resource scarcity, sea level rise, and extreme weather events. These environmental issues can intensify hostilities and force people to relocate, creating security threats and humanitarian emergencies. Global accords such as the Paris Agreement emphasize the necessity of a coordinated approach to reduce the effects of climate change and adjust to its consequences. Together, countries can create resilient plans to protect their infrastructure and people from climate-related risks.

The COVID-19 pandemic has brought to light the significance of worldwide collaboration in defense planning, as evidenced by other pandemics. A coordinated international response is necessary to effectively manage public health emergencies due to the rapid spread of infectious illnesses. Pandemic tracking, containment, and combat activities rely heavily on coordinating efforts by international agencies like the World Health Organization (WHO). Initiatives that work together, such as the COVAX facility, to distribute vaccines fairly show how international collaboration can increase people's ability to withstand health emergencies.

There are still difficulties despite the apparent advantages of global cooperation. Geopolitical rivalry, divergent national interests, and different degrees of commitment can hamper collaboration. The continual problems of bridging capability gaps and guaranteeing that all countries have a stake in collective defense projects need persistent work and diplomacy. Furthermore, resolving trust-related concerns, maintaining transparency, and encouraging inclusive participation in decision-making processes are necessary to develop practical international cooperation.

In conclusion, it is impossible to overestimate the significance of global cooperation in developing a collective defense plan. Modern challenges are interrelated, necessitating a cooperative strategy that uses the resources and strengths of several countries. Countries may create robust defense plans that improve international security by establishing confidence, combining resources, and cooperating through regional and international institutions. The instances of pandemic response, climate change, cybersecurity, and counterterrorism show how teamwork may successfully handle complex security problems. In the future, maintaining a safe and stable world for coming generations will require negotiating the always-changing terrain of global dangers, which will require bolstering international collaboration.

CONCLUSION

The Future of Cybersecurity: Guarding the Digital Frontier: Strategies, Tools, and Best Practices" delves into the complex digital security landscape with a forward-looking perspective. Authored by experts in cybersecurity, the book navigates through evolving threats and cutting-edge defenses essential for safeguarding digital assets.

It starts by examining current cybersecurity challenges, such as data breaches, ransomware attacks, and vulnerabilities in IoT devices, providing real-world examples to illustrate the magnitude of these threats. The authors then pivot to proactive strategies, emphasizing the importance of robust defense mechanisms like encryption, multi-factor authentication, and AI-driven threat detection systems.

Moreover, the book explores emerging technologies poised to shape cybersecurity in the coming years, including quantum computing and blockchain. It goes beyond technical aspects, highlighting the critical role of policy frameworks and international cooperation in addressing global cyber threats.   in

The authors also stress the need for a cybersecurity mindset across all levels of an organization, advocating for continuous education and training to foster a vigilant security culture. By integrating practical advice with theoretical insights, "The Future of Cybersecurity" is a comprehensive guide for cybersecurity professionals and organizational leaders aiming to fortify their defenses against an increasingly sophisticated digital threat landscape.

Thank you for buying and reading/ listening to our book. If you found this book useful/ helpful please take a few minutes and leave a review on the platform where you purchased our book. Your feedback matters greatly to us.

www.ingramcontent.com/pod-product-compliance
Lightning Source LLC
Chambersburg PA
CBHW061316120726
48001CB00002B/535